STANDING
ACCOUNTABLE

Increase Your Success by Holding Yourself
Responsible

Scott Schwab

www.StandingAccountable.com

Copyright 2013 by Scottsdale Book Publishing, LLC

No part of this publication may be reproduced or transmitted in any form or by any means, electronic or mechanical, including photocopy, recording, or any information storage and retrieval system, without permission in writing from the publisher.

ISBN-10: 0983126844

ISBN-13: 978-0-9831268-4-3

Published by:

Scottsdale Book Publishing, LLC

Printed in the United States of America

Contents

Accountability is the greatest and most important skill, trait, and talent. It takes an emotionally stable person to enact all forms of accountability.

Preface

I want to begin this book with a story of how I personally learned accountability and the benefits that it has brought me throughout my life. I grew up in a small farming town in Idaho and enjoyed many of the same activities that other 15-year-old boys enjoy. Football was my passion and something that I spent a lot of time thinking about, dreaming about, and working toward. It was my passion to play at a high level and I was fortunate enough to play with older brothers who made me work hard for every inch.

I was entering my first year of high school as a sophomore and had considerable changes occur physically from my freshman year to the summer before my sophomore year. I remember spending the summer working on a friend's farm doing chores and labor to earn spending money and learn the value of work (my dad's reason). We would wake each morning and walk through miles of barley looking for wild oats that damaged the barley crop. We would walk with potato sacks and fill them with the pulled wild oats and carry them to the end of the field to dump them for pick-up.

The afternoons were spent chasing girls, going bridge jumping, and dreaming with friends. The year before we were in junior high with 8th graders and the new year brought a lot of possibilities. I was excited, not to mention that my physical change had taken me from 5'2" 125 pounds to 5'9" 180 pounds within the year. Surprisingly even with the change of stature I could move well and I was comfortable with the change and was ready for a great year. I had made the change from being the chubby kid to being good sized with some talent.

I grew up in a home with a father who played junior College football and attended Stanford University and a mother who was pageant queen and miss outgoing through her adolescence. I have five brothers and two sisters, and I am fourth of seven. Because of my older siblings, I learned what not to do to stay out of trouble and learned what to do to receive my parents' approval. Additionally, I was able to watch and learn from my older siblings and play sports with them and naturally had to fight for every yard, basket, and point in our neighborhood games.

My parents gave me the best they could and expected the best from me. I was continually reminded that I was special and there were great things in store for me. I bring this up so you can understand the type of upbringing that I had and to paint a picture of who I was. In my youth I was full of energy and definitely the benefactor of a generation and time of pre-diagnosis for ADHD. My mom and dad worked very hard and always had our backs when teachers or community members were critical or from time to time made suggestions about how they needed to control us.

I was a chubby kid with a definite booty. I remember that slim pants were just not in my vocabulary. If you ever asked me what my favorite food was, I would tell you ranch dressing on anything. I was called fat and chubby and my absolute favorite was a rhyme, "Scotty went potty all over his body." Classic. To make matters worse I had a bully named John Walters who for some reason did not want me to exist in his living space. We fought regularly and I may have won a couple but he had most of the victories. Kids on the playground would refer to our epic battles as Andre The Giant Vs. Hulk Hogan, which was probably one of the more favorable compliments in my grade school days.

Honestly I had a great childhood, but there were days that crocodile tears were shed. I did not do well in elementary school and had to meet frequently with a very nice woman, Mrs. Christy, who spent additional time weekly teaching me how to read. My struggle with school continued and it was always a struggle. My parents incentivized me to do well in school, but at times I was punished based on not living up to expectations.

However, sports were my sanctuary. I felt free and everything made sense when I was playing. Most of my days were spent thinking about when I could get home from school and begin my dream of playing in the big leagues. The NFL and even the NBA. My brothers and I also spent quality time building dirt cities in the back yard either in the vacant garden or under our club house. We would set up ramps for our rollerblades and bikes and cruise down the hill toward our house. Needless to say, we all received stitches more than once. Life was very good to me and still continues to be an adventure daily.

Starting my sophomore year of football, there were high hopes and expectations that I was comfortable with. The previous year our lightweight football team easily made it through each game with a win, minus one game with injuries to me and others in key positions. We ended the season with one loss and no tournament to redeem ourselves. The heavyweight team had great talent, and combining our two teams would have made us a powerhouse in Idaho State football. We had raw talent that you find in the fields every morning at 5am moving sprinkler pipe.

We quickly got to work and made our way through "Hell week" with two-a-day practices and heat that reminded you why you were there. I was finding my skills adequate for the positions that I was trying out for. On offense I was trying out for the fullback position, one of blocking and running the ball, lined up directly behind the quarterback. On defense I was looking to start at a linebacker position that would have me in the center of the action. I couldn't have been happier with the upcoming year of promise and glory; or so I thought.

As we started into our third week of practice, we were now fully padded and learning more of the strategy and design of how our team was going to play. We were playing well together and I had secured the positions that I had worked so hard to earn. Monday morning practice arrived and I was excited because in two weeks we would be playing our first game. That coming Friday was also a back-to-school dance and I was looking forward to cutting some rug on the dance floor. As I had grown into my body and had a little more height, I was excited for a new year of living the teenage dream.

Monday's practice came and went without much to note, besides the fact that the team looked great. On Tuesday I noticed a slight pain in my calves and weakness that I could not explain. Wednesday, I had trouble with tackling drills and specifically noting that my legs felt like spaghetti. I also noticed I could not grip anything. Thursday I told my coach that something was wrong and I needed to see the doctor. Upon my visit, tests were run and it was diagnosed that nothing appeared to be wrong and that I was probably sore. However, I could not sprint nor could I do agility drills of any kind so I sat out from practice for Thursday.

Friday came and I remember not being able to move well and feeling like I had to lock my knees to stabilize myself so I could stand or walk. As usual, I had a good friend pick me up and I attended practice in my street clothes. Our practice was on the same practice field as the varsity team. I remember some of the players thinking that I was faking and pushing me down, tripping me, and even throwing me in a puddle of water. I couldn't blame them much because I was a sophomore and I felt as though this was my rite of passage. It was all in good fun and like an owner calling his dogs, the coach eventually called everyone to order and practice began.

By the end of practice I remember being so weak that I could not walk to the car. I had a good friend, Jared Orr, who carried me to the car. That week my mom had been out of town helping my sister Lisa, who had been in a wreck the previous week and was thrown from a Jeep at

65 mph. Miraculously she lived because she landed in a small canal of water.

When I got home from football, my mom burst into tears wondering what had happened to me. I said I had no idea and that I had been to the doctor. She immediately set up a time for me to see another doctor. That night, a tradition was born between my mom and me of watching Harrison Ford movies, while all along I really wanted to be at the dance.

Saturday morning arrived and I went to step out of bed and collapsed on the floor. I was weaker than the day before, and called for my mom, who woke my brother to help me. My mom could not dress me but my little (but stronger) brother could. I still remember us looking at each other with fear in our eyes but no tears because that is something that a 15-year-old and a nearly 14-year-old did not do. He carried me to the van and put me in the front seat. I remember sitting in the van looking at the garage and I can still feel from time to time that feeling of overwhelming "what am I going to do with this?" My mom emerged from the house and we drove the three miles to the doctor's office.

When my mom asked the doctor for a wheelchair, the doctor with a puzzled look asked why. "Scott cannot walk and is unable to use his hands now." He said to get me directly to the ER and that he would call ahead. Because we lived in a smaller town, he instructed my mom to take me to a hospital about 30 minutes away. With that we got in the Ford Windstar and headed for what would be my new home for about three weeks. That may have been the longest 30-minute ride of my life; not because we were in a Ford Windstar. I had taken rides in much slower cars, but this time was different. I didn't seem to feel anything but thoughts in my head.

Once admitted the real fun began and I underwent more tests than I even knew were possible. The attention was intriguing but the mystery of what I had continued to puzzle doctors and neurologists. As the mystery disease continued to climb my body I felt helpless and for the first time abandoned from the inside. I believe this was the first time that I asked "why?" It has taken years to answer that question and I continue to receive insight from time to time, but I am eternally grateful that a boy from nowhere Idaho had the opportunity to grow. This was also the beginning of feelings of resentment and anger. I was not managing my thoughts well as all I could think about was how this would affect my football and my sophomore year.

On the morning of August 27, 1995, I was diagnosed with Guillain-Barre. Guillain-Barre syndrome is a disorder in which the immune system attacks part of the peripheral nervous system. The first symptoms include weakness or tingling sensation in the legs. These feelings can also spread to the arms and upper body. These sensations can increase in severity and a patient can end up paralyzed. This paralysis can interfere with breathing, blood pressure or heart rate. I only had one evening of breathing complications, but the miracle of diagnosis happened and I was now able to be treated. Though hardened and scared of what I was hearing, I was about to go through the most important events of my lifetime.

The second miracle happened as I began to see an outpouring of love from the community, my friends, and the endless support of my family. I found that people cared when at times as a teenager the thought that nobody cares often resonates. However, I found the "why" continually coming into my mind and bitterness setting in. I looked around and saw people looking at me differently, or at least I thought that was the case. I found that girls did not seem to consider me as anything but a friend. I began a cycle of self-defeating thoughts that threatened my happiness and destroyed my confidence.

I was equipped with leg braces that were very stylish if I do say so myself. When I left the hospital I did so in a wheelchair and continued to use the wheelchair for about two months. It was a hard adjustment, but what was even more of an adjustment are functionality activities. Because I could not grip anything I found temporary ways to write. Additionally my dad showered me in the evenings and my mom dressed me in the mornings. I also need to thank the many friends (Shawn, Suzette, Mike, Sam, Ben) who continually gave me rides on a daily basis to and from school. Good friends who actually took me to the bathroom and zipped me up when I was done, popped my zits, and stood up for me at the drop of a hat.

Because of my bitterness and thinking only about myself and how everyone should have pity on me, I found that I pushed a lot of people away and continued to follow a path that I was the victim and anything that happened was a negative event. I began questioning people's motives and stopped believing in the existence of a God. Because if God existed, he surely wouldn't take away the life that I knew and was comfortable with. I have found through the years that my experience gave me that ability to question everything and choose exactly what I wanted out of life. The event that made me question everything was the very event that led me to understanding.

I chose to not only be hurt inside, but to hurt others and feel ok with it. I know it sounds terrible, but at times seeing others hurt when you are hurting makes things feel better temporarily and then immediately worse. The downward spiral is addictive and it seems like nobody understands who you are or what you are going through. Luckily I had good people around me and a supporting cast that no matter how ugly I was to them, they were still beautiful back to me. No matter the nasty things I said, they returned kind words of encouragement to help me see that negativity is not the answer, ever!

The third miracle in looking back at my situation was a father who is a physical therapist. He was ruthless and had me work every day even when I wanted to quit or not show up for treatment. Being inactive caused me to gain a lot of weight and the sedentary lifestyle sure didn't look good with my shirt off. At a time when I was looking for acceptance and positive affirmations, my short-term view of life and only being concerned with my troubles made it very difficult. Every way I turned, I was facing challenges either mentally, physically, emotionally, or spiritually. This difficult time pushed me to the very limit of sanity.

I cannot say that during my teen years I magically learned how to be accountable. However, I can say that this was when I became aware of accountability and started my relationship with learning to be accountable. It has been a step by step, year by year process. I am now comfortable in saying that what happened to me when I was 15 years old was perfect for me and my personal development. At times it is difficult to see the forest through the trees, and other tragedies have come and gone, but the main thing that I have learned is that I am accountable for my thoughts, my words, my actions, and my inactions. Whether we draw something into our life or not, we are responsible for effectively dealing with it and becoming something better. All of us have that ability programmed within us.

It is not easy to improve when there is opposition. However, muscles cannot grow, our minds cannot progress, and our characteristics cannot become defined unless we encounter resistance and opposition.

Our progress, development, and success are tied to our thoughts of who we are and where we fit in the world. Thoughts become our actions and inactions, how we treat others and our daily routines (habits). Our actions become our characteristics of who we ultimately are and what people know of us. Our actions do not necessarily define us, but our characteristics do. It is the difference between the short term and the long term. An action is the short term or the short side of the long term characteristic that we are forming. Whether we recognize it or not, the thoughts that we are planting today will manifest themselves in the future as our character. The simple formula is that our thoughts dictate our actions, and our actions flow into who we are today and who we become tomorrow.

I look forward to sharing my thoughts, beliefs, and perspective with you. Many of the experiences that I have shared are my own; however as a student of life, I continuously look at situations from different angles. I have been fortunate to travel and interact with the average man or woman to the multi-millionaire. Through my interactions and one of my favorite hobbies of people interaction, I do not fear a conversation with anyone. People are people. I once saw Mike Shanahan in a Las Vegas Casino and, throwing caution to the wind, I went up and started a conversation with him. He was amazing and did not take himself or anything else too seriously. I have tried to live by this motto: avoid fear, and let accountability be your guide.

Chapter 1

Accountability and responsibility have a similar theme. Beginning a life or lifestyle with responsibility for something, someone, and ultimately ourselves is an essential step in personal development. Many children benefit from a parent, grandparent, parents who expect their children to find a job, to work, and be responsible for the time allotted to our days or in many cases our summers. Whether it was the chores around the house or the job of mowing the lawns of everyone in the neighborhood, work is a benefactor that blesses everyone.

I may be explaining you when I mention the paper routes that were filled in the early hours of the day and especially on the days that you didn't feel like going to work. Why did you fulfill the responsibility, when you didn't feel like going to work? For all the farm and ranch kids, why did you get up early each morning and work all day for little wages? We all can say we have done something that we did not want to do. This is the first principle of accountability. We must learn that there are certain responsibilities, tasks, and events that we will not want to face nor complete. As we face challenges there is a definable feeling that we will have that confirms that our decision to accept accountability was and is correct.

I remember my parents teaching me accountability and

expecting me to work. My brothers and sisters and I were raised with the idea that if we wanted something, we had to work for it. One of the best jobs in a small farming community was moving pipe and doing other manual labor. My mom and dad also encouraged us to play sports. There were times that I didn't like the job, I didn't like my teams, but it was never an option to quit or discontinue. If I started something, I was going to finish.

I worked on a farm, where I and my friend Spencer Fullmer would talk daily about quitting. The oldest son Brian, who was mostly our boss, was a jerk to put it lightly. He criticized us, demeaned, and yelled to get his point across. There were many times he hurt my feelings and I wanted to cry and I probably did. However, I never quit and actually we became good friends. I consider that time as pivotal for shaping my life and helping me learn many of life's lessons that still help me today.

Growing up, my dad worked us hard, but as I look back, he probably did 80% of the work. My mom tried to make work fun, and Saturdays were filled with cleaning and music by Chicago and Journey blaring out of our windows. My foundation for accountability in many ways was developed from the need and expectation to do my part and participate in work. My parents taught me hard work, honor, duty, and to never quit. They lived by the mantra "Schwabs don't quit" and that was drilled into my head during all of my adolescence.

In speaking of feelings, it is also true that we can feel the stress of a situation or the pressure of having to deal with an uncomfortable scenario. Think about how you would deal with this situation:

You have invited a friend over for dinner. The friend has confirmed their attendance and a time has been set for their arrival. Meanwhile, the friend who accepted the invitation has received another invitation to a party. A larger group would be gathering, and for all intents and purposes, it could be a more desirable situation.

What do you do?

All of us have been in this situation in some form or another. We may experience this in our professions, dating, relationships, or family responsibilities. At a deeper level, we have all experienced this from the grand question of right and wrong, people's perceptions, expectations, and even our own thoughts of what we desire. All of these emotions, thoughts, and feelings are occurring, often within seconds of a decision being made. At the subconscious level our body will start feeling the pressure before we even think about what to do. Our bodies will do this in the form of uncomfortable feelings in our stomach, perspiration, and even body aches long before our conscious mind begins to think through the situation. We can and will recall these scenarios as we have hindsight of 20/20 and sort through the situation.

Now, back to our example; as we put ourselves in the shoes of the original person extending the invitation, we need to think about the preparation. Likely the person has prepared something for the dinner and if there are others, there has been time put into other invitations. There may be cost in reference to the meal. There have likely been time adjustments made so that the dinner could be at a mutually desired time. Cleaning and other activities could be a part of the equation and in general we should consider the feelings of the host.

As the person who has been invited, there are multiple options, and options are good. However, it now comes down to simple communication and commitment. If we value the thoughts and feelings of others, we will stick to our original commitment because we freely made that decision on our own. If we live based on what is going to be most enjoyable, we may make a decision that will create excuses and justifications that secure the decision to make it right in our mind. Justification is a very dangerous tool, and will not only take us from doing what is right, but opens doors to more justification and a lack of self-discipline.

Our commitment is the only real thing we have at the end of the day. When the people are gone, the money is irrelevant, and we are one-on-one with the mirror, we are only as good as our commitments that we have kept. Justification on the other hand gives us a false sense of security and superiority that our decision making is correct. It will not matter whether something is right or wrong, justification is a habit and if we do not have the self-discipline to live by commitment, our life will be a continuous battle of staying true to self or letting self create our own truth. Justification will do just that. Truth is not truth when we are twisting the reasons for our decisions.

The example above is just an example and though it can tell us a lot about ourselves based on our answer, it also does not define who we are. The age old story of nature vs. nurture is a more applicable gauge of where we stand in our decision making process. All of us were raised in conditions that may or may not be ideal. Regardless of how we were raised, our perception of ourselves and the world we live in becomes our reality. There are many stories of people who lived in terrible circumstances and emerged as powerful individuals who have done much good. There are also stories of people who had it all, but did nothing to build themselves or others.

Let's be clear that money does not buy happiness or provide the ideal life. My favorite story of a person who overcame serious odds and has become an individual for change is Oprah Winfrey. She has emerged from a life of literal terror, abuse, and contempt that many of us including me would never understand. She stands as an example that great things can come from the seemingly impossible.

Nurture could be defined by the way we are raised. Not only what we see others do, but also the circumstances of our mind and the confidence we gain through situations. Life is made of the good, the bad, and even ugly situations that we can either choose to learn from or become the victim to the situation. Unfortunately, all of us have played the victim at some point in our life. Fortunately though, we all have the opportunity to build our character and become a person who fully embraces accountability. Nurture could also be defined from the way we are raised, but more appropriately takes into account the decisions we make and ultimately how we choose to live.

We nurture our character by the things we think about, the actions that are born from our thoughts, and finally the consistency that creates the foundation of our character. Our character is a composite of people we have watched, experiences we have had, but completely relies on the decisions that we make. It is our decision to focus on what nurtures us. It may not be our nature to be accountable for our decisions, but we are not justified in that. Nurture on the other hand is how we come programmed. I say it that way because as a father of three our children are very very different. They, like us, are all individuals, and we must treat our children and people as individuals.

A person cannot build a strong foundation for life if the response to anything is, "that is the way I was raised." That statement takes the power of choice out of the equation. We are not justified in becoming the people we are because we were raised in a difficult circumstance. A very good friend of mine was subject to abuse in continual but temporary living conditions with drugs and a stepmother who continually told him he was worthless. My friend has two brothers who have chosen to live a life with drugs and have continually been in and out of jail. Matt, on the other hand, has emerged as the champion of his destiny. Though he hasn't had a perfect life laced with only good things, he has turned the potential bad into lessons for life and continues to build others by building himself.

I believe that a person regardless of their place in life needs two things. #1 People need a voice. I am not talking about a singing voice or a voice that is pleasant to listen to. I am speaking about a voice where a person can be listened to. To have a person or people in their life who listens to them and validates their thoughts, goals, opinions, and dreams. I will also refer to this concept of voice as validation. #2 The second essential thing that a person needs is acceptance. Just because we have a person who will listen to us does not mean we have acceptance. People seek acceptance their whole lives and will find it in many places. Religion, support groups, sports, activities, hobbies, and even our vocation can all represent a form of acceptance.

We desire to have people surrounding us who have similarities that allow us to feel like we are not alone. This may come in the form of people who think alike, look alike, have the same hobbies, enjoy the same entertainment, etc. When we really sit and think about it, there are many ways of connecting. Realize, though, those we choose to associate with become the average of our earnings, our lifestyle, and will often make up our ability to be accountable. Although we have the final say with our choice of accountability, it is essential that we choose people who share our feelings on life and accountability.

The two most powerful feelings are love and fear. Fear comes from feelings of discomfort, danger, and lack of preparation. Love comes from feelings of trust, confidence, loyalty, and devotion. Both feelings flow into accountability and can create a higher level of joyful living. As individuals, if we simply were accountable for our thoughts, our feelings, and our actions, life would become much simpler. Our interactions would be pure and people who interact with us would know exactly where we stand. There would be no doubt of responsibility or our character.

We would not need to spend time making excuses or thinking of reasons why a situation unfolded as it did. This consistency would also naturally allow others to make similar decisions of taking responsibility. Commitment would never be questioned because those who live their lives accountable also live their lives with more satisfaction. When we think about the things that bring sorrow in life, every single situation could be resolved if a person or people would take accountability. Accountability brings with it a pressure to do the right thing and make the choice that empowers rather than hinders.

It also must be mentioned that just because a person lives their life accountable, their life will not be perfect. Perfection is a quest that none will achieve. Those who live a life of accountability will realize this and make the necessary adjustments to live a happy life despite imperfections. When we think about accountability in all of its forms, it really comes down to each of us making the commitment to accept the thoughts that we choose to have in our mind. We also choose that accountability drives our decisions and will always affect others because actions will always influence others. Finally, our accountability for character and our quest of becoming who we desire is built upon the foundation of choice, reason, and accountability.

Accountability is commitment and commitment is accountability. These exist in the same sphere of taking responsibility for our thoughts, actions and character. If we can choose to act rather than be acted upon, we have begun building our foundation that will bring success and opportunity in abundance. Again, opportunity does not always mean positive situations. It does however mean that a person will take whatever the situation is and make it into a positive outcome. Accountability is our ability to take control of our lives and pass on the hope of empowerment through accountability to others.

> "To each there comes in their lifetime a special moment when they are figuratively tapped on the shoulder and offered the chance to do a very special thing, unique to them and fitted to their talents. What a tragedy if that moment finds them unprepared or unqualified for that which could have been their finest hour."
>
> *-Winston Churchill-*

Chapter 2

Continually we see evidences of a declining society all around us. Unfortunately, based on our attraction to media and the obvious increases in the information age, we see these effects spilling into ethics, our relationships, and our homes. The internet has brought about so many positive things; however, the increase of knowledge also increases the probability of finding the lewd, the lascivious, and the decadent. Our familiarity and exposure has our society dumbed down to the world around us.

In true fashion, the ultimate accountability measure is not to blame our environmental or external surroundings but to live great in the face of mediocrity. Though there are more opportunities to find evidences of a declining society, this would mean that naturally there are also more opportunities to do good, be great, and live exceptionally. Living great is a choice and those who choose accountability over victim thinking, excuse making, and justification will live closer to greatness no matter their personal or financial outcomes. Accountability requires growth because it requires change and a constant awareness that we can make a difference in our lives and the lives of others by accepting what we think, say, and do.

The world around us is changing fast and ultimately we see people's perception as their reality. However, what is it that guides our perceptions? Our perceptions are guided by Nature and Nurture. How we choose to see the world, in many ways, is the way that we choose to explain our involvement in the world. If all we know is hurt, pain, and sorrow, our perception is that the world is a hurtful, painful place. One person may have been born in totally different circumstances and will not ever experience exactly what another person may experience. However, regardless of who you are or where you are from, you will experience some level of hurt, pain, and sorrow in your lifetime. In my own life, I remember the days of hurting emotionally because of the limits of my mind and body from the effects of Guillain-Barre. I hurt inside and as bad as it sounds, I wanted other to know my pain and experience hurt like I was feeling. I viewed the experience as unfair and because I viewed others as not experiencing the same thing, in a very sad way I wanted others to hurt.

To those whom I hurt or was unkind to, I apologize and wish that I could take those words and actions back. I especially feel bad for my family and friends who seemed to get the brunt of the abuse. Unfortunately my immaturities lead me to say things and do things during these years that were unkind. I found out that this short-term understanding did not bring happiness at all, but actually made me feel worse. It is not my job or yours to make sure that a person is punished or learns a lesson. Those lessons come all on their own and I firmly believe that karma will find all of us.

We have no right to discredit another person's experience, but can only validate the experience and ultimately ourselves based on whether we listen and have empathy and understanding. The other validation that often occurs is the judgment that is passed. This act unfortunately does not validate the person at all, but more appropriately defines the ignorance and insensitive nature of the person passing judgment. To be able to experience life to the fullest, we must feel what others feel, we must consider what others think, and we must not pass judgment without understanding. The old saying goes: "Don't judge a man until you have walked a mile in his shoes."

If we are to progress and learn more about ourselves, we need to learn more about others. By identifying traits, personalities, and characteristics flaws in others; we often times will identify those same traits within ourselves. Often times we will point out criticisms in others that we are familiar with, can identify with, and find within ourselves. So before we look at others with the intent to criticize or bring down another person, let us try to understand where they are coming from and why they think the way they do. In this way we are better prepared to respond to challenges we will face, and situations where simply taking a higher road or incorporating a better response will change the outcome of the events we encounter.

Accountability begins within the homes and with who the teaching is coming from. It is a parent's role to provide guidance, understanding, and teachings for children born to them. Unfortunately the majority of men and women can produce children, but this does not make the man or the woman. Reproductive responsibility should be done in an environment where there is equal understanding, shared love, and, more than anything, accountability for that child and the rearing of the child. The New York Times reported that over half of births are now performed by single mothers under 30 and outside of marriage.

In our increasing world that is eliminating the middle class and spreading the gap between the rich and poor, single parents have a much more difficult responsibility than in times past. Children need role models, parents, grandparents, and a community that will help shape their future role and define their views on the world. Divorce is another problem that negatively affects children, adults, and communities. It is estimated that one-third of divorcees regret their decision to split from their spouse (www.unitedfamilies.org). Children of divorces have perhaps the most difficult time identifying with the world, their peers, and will often times blame themselves for the divorce. This is the reality even when parents and society try to convince the child otherwise.

Statistically, educational success and vocational satisfaction are higher in homes of families. Additionally, children are more likely to be involved in crime and drop out of school when parents are not present and there is not a defined role model in their lives (http://www.ncbi.nlm.nih.gov/pmc/articles/PMC2853053/). Values are taught by good people everywhere, but they are learned best when they are lived by the parents and guardians who raise the children. Often times our actions are so loud that the words we speak have no sound. Keeping commitments and being accountable are the biggest source for growth and progress that future generations can benefit from.

Illiteracy in America continues to climb and one of the biggest forms of a declining society is illiteracy. When we consider what is allowed in our homes; do we read books and have our children read books? A Nielsen Report recently revealed that the average American spends 34 hours per week watching live television. Another 3-6 hours are spent watching recorded shows. This is nearly a day and a half of 7 days spent watching television. With this much time being spent in front of the television, it is no wonder that books are becoming an endangered species. According to the National Literacy Survey, 42 million adult Americans can't read; 50 million can recognize so few printed words they are limited to a 4th or 5th grade reading level. One out of every four teenagers drops out of high school, and of those who graduate, one out of every four has the equivalent or less of an eighth grade education.

Gaming has also become something on the rise with homes that have consoles. Gaming accounts for as much or more time than what is spent watching television according to a Michigan State study. Additionally, researchers at Indiana University report that brain scans show that violent video games can alter brain function in healthy young men after just a week of play, depressing activity among regions associated with emotional control. Other studies have found an association between compulsive gaming and being overweight, introverted and prone to depression (www.ncbi.nlm.nih.gov/pubmed/19006465).

Since the release of "World of Warcraft" in 2004, the registered online users have accounted for 50 billion hours, which adds up to 5.9 million years. Is there any need to argue the point of what is really going on in our country?

By making changes in our homes and keeping commitments to one another, we change society. What do we let inside our homes by way of television, internet, or radio? If the media portrays life inconsistent with our values, the effect is that we take a stand and we do not allow them in our homes. Children are intelligent and when we do not stand up for things we say or do, children are more likely to forgo taking a stand in their own lives. Furthermore, consequences or accountability must be taught to our children and communities. Many times adolescent mistakes are made because there is not a clear understanding of consequences. Teaching cause and effect is valuable for the future of every child in every home.

Another problem that seems to be removing children from accountability is parents' inability to let the child face their consequences. As parents, we want our children to have the very best and avoid as much pain and sorrow as possible. We cripple our children when we remove them from accountability. Taking them away from decisions only solidifies the knowledge that a child will easily escape any poor decisions that they make in their lives. Though it may be difficult, we must let our children learn responsibility even in the face of embarrassment, humiliation, and natural consequences. When we help children learn responsibility and live accountably, we change our homes, our communities, and our world.

I remember my first encounter with accountability. I was seven years old and had decided that it was time for me to get some bubble tape chewing gum. The only problem is that I had no money. Never before had I considered stealing, but today was the day that I cared more about obtaining what I wanted than working for it. I knew theft was wrong. I had been taught that my whole life. After I walked the two miles to Maverick and took the gum, I started my walk home. The remorse of the situation hadn't set in and in fact I think I had put the whole bubble gum tape roll in my mouth.

Life was great until my older brother Travis picked me up on the side of the road with his friends. He asked me where I got the gum. I said that I bought it. He said, "With what money?" I was caught and he knew I was busted. In fact, those were the very words he used. He told my mom. My mom said I would need to wait for my dad to get home. My dad was a very nice man, but when you stepped out of line, you were in for it. I remember the scolding well, but the biggest impression was the feeling of my heart dropping when he said to get in the car because we were going to take care of it. I didn't know what that meant until we pulled up to Maverick.

My dad had me come in the store and apologize to the store clerk. He then pulled out his wallet and paid for the gum. I remember that it was quite the scene or at least it felt like all eyes in the store were on me. To me it seemed that all of Rexburg was there, when in reality it may have been 10 people. Consequently I spent the next couple of months paying off what seemed to be 20 packs worth of bubble tape. Whenever my dad needed something, I was there as his sidekick. At first he had to remind me that I was paying off the debt, but as we continued to do work together, he encouraged my accountable participation.

I appreciate that experience as my first opportunity to feel accountable. Those feelings continued with trips to Island Park to cut wood for our wood-burning fire stove to stock up for winter. It didn't matter if I wanted to go, I was going. My dad made it worth it though with trips to Maverick and we were able to get a burger and a Fat Boy ice cream sandwich. Maverick was just a part of my dad's routine and rightfully so as Rexburg didn't have many other options.

If we do not learn from our past, we cannot provide a better future. Most likely, each of us has made mistakes that vary in degree of seriousness. Take the time right now to reflect and do a personal accounting for our thoughts, words, and actions. Are we living accountable in each of these areas? Based on our mistakes, we can help identify paths and actions for our children, our community, our co-workers, our spouse, and our world. When accountability is present, we take on the additional responsibility to guide and help others. It is not that we always spend our time correcting others, but that we provide a model for what accountability is, we serve as the listening ear to others, and we give sound advice that a mentor would give. The role of the accountable truly is the role of a mentor.

It only takes one person standing up for something to change the perception of what others will believe in.

There have been many great causes that have changed our world and made this time the most incredible time to live. We will live the dreams of past generations and dreaming we must do. Passing on this belief is an arduous task that will not always manifest results.

It is much like the story of the ugly duckling. The world chose to look at the ugly duckling one way with harsh remarks and insults that hurt the ugly duckling's feelings. As he set out on his own, additional challenges mounted and the ugly duckling continued to look for acceptance. As the story is coming to a close with the ugly duckling, he finally decides to accept his situation and interact with the swan in the pond, even if it means that he will lose his life.

Eventually, as other stories go regarding potential, the ugly duckling eventually grows up and realizes he is a beautiful swan. Accepted by others, he finds his place in the world and takes flight with his new family. There are many lessons such as persistence, resilience, and a will to live, that can be learned from this story. One lesson that I believe is critical to all of our understanding is the lesson of acceptance. It seems that the ugly duckling searched everywhere for acceptance, but eventually found it because of his growth and maturity. Is this not the same with human interaction? We search our whole lives for acceptance, yet all we may need is growth and maturity.

That growth and maturity comes through accountability. We need to ask ourselves" is acceptance really that strong of a motivator? Look at the world and you be the judge. Is this not evident by the choices of society and even our individual decisions? As we discussed in Chapter 1, a person is in need of a voice (validation) and acceptance. A person will search night and day until they find both and can be comfortable with the feeling of belonging.

Is acceptance really that strong of a motivator? Look at the world and you be the judge. Is this not evident by the choices of society and even our individual decisions? As we discussed in Chapter 1, a person is in need of a voice (validation) and acceptance. A person will search night and day until they find both and can be comfortable with the feeling of belonging.

This journey is often most recognizable in children, as they search for acceptance within a group, among friends, or even online. This really does not change much as we age and the same desires are often sought in the form of religion, society, organizations, etc. We all know people in our life who will do anything for acceptance. How do you seek acceptance and validation in your life? The desire to be noticed and feel accepted is very real for each of us. Validation, on the other hand, is also important as this relates not only to the group, but having a voice within the group. One cannot truly be part of a group without participation in one form or another. Acceptance is only half of the equation as it is necessary to feel part of the group based on contribution or at least being listened to.

Each of our needs are as unique as our DNA. All of us seek certain types of living based on our hopes, dreams, and faith to achieve the desired outcome. Whether you refer to outcomes based on faith or reality, it is the same. Our ability to create starts with a thought or "faith" that we can achieve. We choose our reality based on how we think and specifically what we think about. This idea will be covered in greater detail in Chapter 4 with the setting of goals.

As a way of review; we are the key to our society. By taking a stand we can make a difference. If we choose not to take a stand, we will continue to see the evidence of a struggling society. Accountability is the necessary step to reverse current trends and offer the solutions for the problems we face today. To prevent the downward spiral of the society as a whole, we must provide the direction for an alternative. The alternative is you, it is me, it is accountability.

"To uncover your true potential, you must first find your own limits and then you have to have the courage to blow past them."

-*Picabo Street*-

Chapter 3

Often times we like to discuss the problems and not offer the solutions. We may not realize it, but this is not only about attitude. It is more about accountability. Accountability requires us to think past the problem and create a solution. When we only focus on problems, we create the reflection of being a victim of the circumstances. Victim thinking, like fear, debilitates or serves as a paralysis to action. When we exhibit victim minded thinking, we are in essence giving away our will to act. We spend so much time finding blame, making excuses, and enjoying pity from others that we often miss the opportunity for growth. I like to refer to the choice of Accountability vs. Victim thinking in a model I refer to as the 3 R's for revolution.

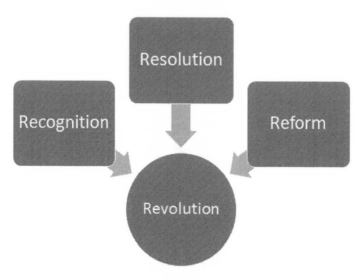

THE 3 R's FOR REVOLUTION

The first step that each of us must do in our progress is **recognition**. We must recognize that there is a problem and what our involvement might be in the situation. Until we can understand our involvement, we may not clearly understand a solution. The second step is an action step of **resolution**. This is not only to think of possible solutions to the problem, but this is a step forward to <u>act</u> and <u>stand</u> for what we believe the outcome should be. Remember the step of creating starts with a thought, progresses to our voice, and continues with an action. Resolution comes from the study of what to do. The final step is to **reform**. When we reform, we do not just repeat; we remove the defect. This is also known as pivoting, adjusting, and adapting. Repeating the same thing and expecting different results is insanity.

When we repeat an action and remove the defect we begin to see the world from a different point of view. Often times these points of view come from meditating or studying in our minds the solution. We also gain perspective by speaking with others who are not as close to the situation and getting feedback. At times, we must step back and look at the problem from a balcony view. Effective solutions come when we have exhausted the obvious. This does not mean that we spend an excessive amount of time looking for a decision. This means we trust our instincts and the reasoning that we have gained through experience.

A great book that I highly recommend is by Malcolm

Gladwell, called Blink. In the book he looks at the relationship between our ability to make decisions according to our instincts rather than getting bogged down with details and opinions from others. He points out that we negatively affect our ability to respond when we try to analyze and overthink situations.

Decisions and choice frequently involve change, which is difficult for many people. The fear of change comes from the unknown, giving up the pleasant, and the inconvenience of change itself. At the root of change sprouts our ability to respond. Response and perception are important for change and both are exhibited either through Accountability or Victim thinking. When we think about the 3 R's for revolution let's compare the possible responses to the example below.

Example:

Unfortunately layoffs are occurring at the company that you work for. Each department is letting go a couple of individuals. As employees find out about the layoffs there are many ideas as to how the layoffs will occur. It becomes such a discussion around the water cooler that there is a very negative feeling about the company and the direction they are choosing to go.

There are many different responses that a person could have in this situation. Many of these feelings could be justified, and likely anger, fear, and misunderstanding are a part of these feelings. Regardless of whether you stay at the company or you are laid off, choose the response that best portrays your attitude.

Stay:

"This is a great opportunity to take on additional responsibilities and show my additional value. I have a lot to offer and despite the terrible situation, I choose to be positive about the situation."

"All my friends have been laid off. I don't understand why the company is doing this. They have plenty of profits and maybe the CEO should pay himself less and they could have saved the jobs they cut. I will probably be laid off as well so I might as well look for another job too."

Laid Off:

"People get laid off and unfortunately I was selected. However, I have gained great experience and feel like I have a lot to offer. The job market is tough, but I am tougher. I will work that much harder to find a situation where I can succeed."

"Why does this always happen to me? I have given the past 2 years to that company and for what? The job market is terrible and I probably won't find a job. What am I going to do? I have a mortgage, bills, and now I don't have a job. Life sucks."

There is an obvious difference between the two responses. This situation is a reality for many people and our response and perception is crucial to our psyche and the ability to act. One of the biggest problems we have is that we spend so much time listening to ourselves rather than telling ourselves what we need to do. The process of creating an outcome is more powerful than when we merely respond to the situation. Negative or positive, both live within the confines of our mind. It is important to recognize this because many times we listen to the negative rather than choosing to be positive. Average lives within each of us and we all can respond with the typical, I can't, I won't, I'm not good, nobody loves me, etc. These are normal responses, however, they are not justified or appropriate.

I experienced this in 2010 when I was fired. Both responses were something that I had a chance to experience. I was hired as a consultant for a company located in Vancouver, Washington. I met my boss and owner of the firm while on a plane. At the time I was a Regional Sales Manager with a door to door marketing firm. We marketed pest control products and I was traveling between San Diego and Portland. I sat next to Mark and we clicked very quickly.

Over the course of the next month we went through continual phone conversations, in person interviews, and email exchange. I was hired and quickly started a commute from Utah to Portland for training as well as learning the ropes. We worked with companies like Adidas and other large organizations in developing leadership and management curriculums. It was the dream job and

I really enjoyed the work. My job was to build business in Utah. With my sales background, I felt this would be a semi-simple task.

However, I quickly realized the difficulty and wasn't getting the results that Mark or I had expected or projected. I tried getting guidance and suggestions, and Mark's response was that he didn't have time to teach me everything that he knew, he expected an experienced salesman to go make it happen and create business. My lack of knowledge outweighed my excitement and desire to succeed. Six short weeks after I was hired, I was called on the phone and fired. It was hard to face the fact that I didn't live up to the expectation of the job. I went through a time of self-doubt and spent time beating myself up. However, I had to make the decision to learn from the past and stop living in the regrets of yesterday.

When we spend the majority of our time listening to these inner negative responses, what do you think our actions or inactions will be? The outcome is dictated by how we choose to respond. If we listen to the "I can't" or "I won't," do you believe the result will be any different? Victim thinking will cause fear and ultimately produce a non-response.

"Whether you think you can or you think you can't…. you are probably right."

-Henry Ford-

Now think about the positive or encouraging words of "I can" and "I will." The response is much different and alone will empower our thoughts, words, and actions. Our response will change our perception and further influence a positive outcome. The outcome becomes positive because we chose Accountability. As opposed to fear, distrust, and negativity that come from Victim thinking. I believe that all forms of fear, hate, derogatory remarks, and violence come from a threat either actual or perceived. Victim thinking is selfish thinking because we are only responding to what would serve us best. Whereas with accountability, we seek for a favorable outcome for everyone involved. Let me clarify, this does not mean that we always choose to back down so there is not confrontation. It means that we choose what we believe in and take a firm stance while accepting the input of others based on a choice to learn from interaction.

Victim thinking can be compared to emotional responses to situations. When we allow emotions to dictate our responses, we can say and do things that truly do not represent our character. As we ascend the straight path of accountability, we determine our responses based on our level of self-awareness and who we really are at the core. We do not let situations define our characters. We define our characters and let situations be what they are. This way of thinking may be a large change or a small change in our lives. Some of the most captivating knowledge comes from meditation and allowing ourselves to read great books, think, reason, and respond. In our society we are inundated with media that paints a picture of selfishness and greed. Movies, television shows, and the news do not confirm truth. Rather media would inform us that somewhere in the world this is the way we should think, act, and do. Though it may be appealing or possibly cast fear that paralyzes, we must avoid the proddings to be something we are not.

When looking at the events that happen in life, we know that there will be times in life when mistakes happen. One of the most sure ways that a victim mind can be recognized is when events such as mistakes happen. Mistakes are determined simply by how we choose to learn from the event. We can make excuses, blame others, choose not to face the issue, or we can choose to face the event and grow. Mistakes are determined by how we process the information in our minds. The victim mind will choose to feel like he or she has been cheated or has no control, rather than choosing growth and opportunity which is realized by the accountable mind.

A great book that I would recommend reading is The Ownership Spirit by Dennis Deaton. His book identifies victim minded thinking and provides suggestions that we can implement to overcome such thinking. He finishes his book with stories of many who have endured challenging things and, in the face of great trials, chose to take the higher road of response. It is increasingly clear that the changes that are needed do not come from the solutions that solved earlier problems alone. The ability to overcome the problems of today and tomorrow will come through the process of analysis from the past and a stance to think, to speak, and to act accountable today. Accountability controls our capacity to feel and thus predicts our behavior. Ultimately we make the choice of whether we will be the victim of our circumstances or choose accountability despite the circumstances.

"Everything you want in life is located just outside of your comfort zone."

-Robert Allen-

Chapter 4

Goal setting is one of the most powerful tools that we can possess but the most misunderstood resource. A goal is not a wish and it is not a desire alone. A goal is a detailed process for attainment. Whether this process exists in our mind or we have put our thoughts to paper, a goal is a plan. The areas that cause the most stress and frustration for people are goals that cannot or will not be obtained. The highest factors for consideration of non-obtainable goals can be broken down into three major areas:

1. Misunderstanding of the goal, requirements, and fulfillment needed.

2. Misjudgment between Results and Performance or in other words breaking down the goal into a series of accomplishments.

3. Lack of commitment, follow-through, and confidence.

When considering each of these areas, accountability alone solves the immediate and long term requirements. However, an even greater aspect is knowledge and understanding. We cannot be accountable if we simply do not understand a concept, principle, or performance. When we look at goal setting and accountability, we are setting goals that we would like to accomplish. Most often we begin the steps toward completion only to find that the goal is more difficult than expected. It should be understood that a goal is most often going to be something that will challenge our current status which constitutes the need for change and adjustment.

A great way of looking at a goal and keeping things simple is an acronym that is used in management. The **S.M.A.R.T.** goal concept was created in 1981 by George Doran, Arthur Miller, and James Cunningham. It was originally used as a tool to help management set goals and objectives, but is widely accepted today for accurately looking at goals and the steps needed to obtain those goals.

S. Specific – Make your goals specific so that they are not just desires or dreams.

M. Measurable – A goal should be tracked and represent a clear way of understanding progress and areas for improvement.

A. Achievable – Goals are set to drive achievement and not frustration. Set goals that you can achieve knowing it will require work.

R. Realistic – Setting goals should reflect the amount of work that you are willing to put into achievement.

T. Time Based – This ties into the measurement of the goal. A correct time frame will represent realistic achievement not an unrealistic hope that does not include work.

"Remember, when you talk about something, it's a dream. When you envision it, it's exciting. When you plan it, it's possible. But, when you schedule it, it's real."

-Anthony Robbins-

One thing that is important for goal setting is to focus on where you are currently and how you personally can improve, rather than comparing yourself to others and wondering why you're not where they are. Goal setting, and goal attainment for that matter, is the reflection of what you are willing to work for and what you truly desire. It is not simply to have what someone else has or become what someone else is.

During my life, I have lived the model of trying to compare myself to others and hope that I could have the success that they had. Trying to be what I am not and through expectations of others, spending a lot of time trying to convince myself and others of my value. I believe we can all relate to this challenge and probably notice that we may embellish or fabricate what we are doing or have done based on our perception of where we want to be or think we should be. The need to be accepted often times outweighs our ability to accurately reason.

There is a saying that is prominent in society that I think often times does more harm than good, and definitely challenges accountability. "Fake it until you make it." Another popular form of this is the Self-fulfilling prophecy originated by Robert K. Murton. Finally, William James coined the phrase "Act as if." The difference is intent and deceit. Obviously there are levels of deceit; however, I have learned the value of not telling everything that I would like to do and what I have plans to do and just communicating the things that are done. It is important to dream, and I am a dreamer. It is valuable to stretch our mind about what is possible and then use the reality component of getting to work.

In my twenties it was so important for me to tell everyone all the things that I was doing or was going to do. I realized how annoying this may have been and found people giving me the look like, "here we go again." It became very real when a friend asked me when I was going to stop talking about all the ideas I had and complete one of them. That gentle prompting helped me to shut my mouth and get to work. Accountability is not talk, it is action. Regardless of how we think we must present our lives, it is better to be accurate than illusive.

I would now like to look at a goal that I believe each of us has either made or knows someone who has made. Weight loss is the biggest resolution that is made in America each year (University of Scranton, Journal of Clinical Psychology 12.13.2012). The ironic thing is that by February most people have abandoned their goals and moved comfortably back to their pre-resolution status. This is interesting because the goal represented a need and a want, but the short-term results often dictate the decision to continue or to quit. That is why we should not focus on the outcome or desired results alone, but the steps or performance of getting there. For a goal to be successful, we must internalize it or create it mentally before we perform physically.

The same steps or process exists in our minds before we take the first step of action. I submit that one of the key areas for goal attainment is to write down our goals and commit our behavior to them. Simply having a goal in mind or a desire is not enough, because there are so many other things on our minds or situations that require an action. If we make our goals situational, we fail. What I mean by this is simply having a wish to lose weight fails when we are out with our friends some evening, or when we have worked all day and have no energy. Furthermore, our habits will confront our desired behavior; we must learn to make a choice. Remember, if we have written something down and committed it to our way of doing and being, we are much more likely to become.

The process of doing, being, and becoming is best accomplished when we focus on behavior as opposed to habits. Our habits are what we currently have based on our thoughts, words, actions and inactions, which become our habits and our character. To be successful in goal attainment, we must understand that we will challenge the very habit and character that we have created. Success in any goal will require a challenge and a change or adjustment. The behavior we desire must be a planned effort. For instance, if we look to the situations we often find ourselves in, we must understand that if we are a smoker and want to quit, we must avoid situations where there will be smoke and smokers. If we are trying to quit drinking alcohol, we should avoid bars and other social situations that present the challenge.

Planning is an essential area for focus with any goal. A helpful saying that helps when thinking about planning is to remember the 5 P's. Proper preparation prevents poor performance. As discussed before, our first plan begins within our mind as a desire. This is our subconscious flowing into our conscious. At that very point that we have the conscious thought for change, we must take a new step forward of action or possibly inaction, if our desire is to discontinue something.

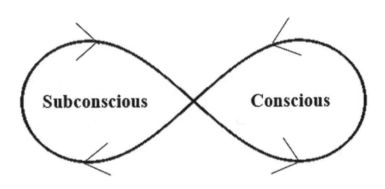

Example 4.1: Subconscious to Conscious flow

For sustainable success, we must write down the goals or the results that we desire. During this same session of writing down our goals or the results we desire, we need to write down our performance or the short-term actions needed for the desired results or the long-term goal attainment. Success will have us break down the goal into a series of time frames. Within those time frames will emerge fractions of the total goal broken down into equal increments until we reach our goal and our long-term result. This is known as measuring and relates to performance.

A well-known statistician, author, lecturer, and consultant, William Edwards Demming, looked at the world from the viewpoint of systems, processes, and knowledge obtained from the system or process. I refer to him here, because if there ever was a system or process, goal setting and goal attainment fits the category. He is credited with much of the Japanese success in manufacturing and business. He consistently taught principles of improvement and development through adjustments. He taught the principle that, "If you cannot measure it, you cannot manage it."

Dr. Demming introduced the cycle named after him, which also has been referred to as the Shewhart cycle. The method was designed to test information before making a major decision. I want to take the Demming Model and apply it to the goal setting aspect. The main aspect that applies to goal setting is the steps taken toward accountability. The four major steps in the Demming cycle are: Plan-Do-Check-Act (PDCA).

Think of your goal as your Plan. The next step is to Do what you originally thought would be required using discovery to yield an outcome. Check to see if you are on track with your goal and align your goal to the outcome or result. Action is the final step which is the most important and represents the goal attainment. The final step of action also takes into account what was learned along the way and represents a calculated action. The PDCA cycle is a perfect way to see if the goals you are setting will bring you the outcome you are hoping for, while raising the level of understanding. Perhaps a new direction should be taken, or your original thoughts are validated by the process.

Remember that input will dictate the outcome. The idea and creation of the goal within our mind is often the easiest in the process. We cannot forget the process of action by putting our thoughts into reality. Reality does require work and by learning through applying, we can be taught a better way for achieving what we had hoped for in our mind as we intially started our journey of the idea. Be patient with yourself, because often times you will be facing something uncomfortable, unfamiliar, and more than likely a change from the norm. Putting uneeded stress upon yourself only hinders performance, so learn to work with pressure, but not with stress.

Example 4.2: The diagram below will help explain the cycle as it applies to setting and obtaining goals.

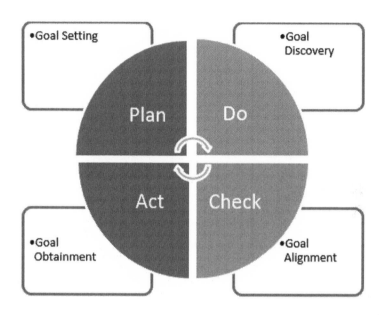

•Goal Setting

•Goal Discovery

Plan

Do

Act

Check

•Goal Obtainment

•Goal Alignment

Example:

You have hired a person to perform a task or job for you. When you originally speak about the task, there is a clear understanding of what you are willing to pay. The person accepts and begins the task. As he works, he finds the task more difficult and that it takes longer than he expected. Upon completion, the person tells you that the job was more difficult than expected so he should receive more wages.

With this in mind, think through the process and respond with what you would do.

Now, imagine that this conversation took place on the phone. You told this person to go to your place of business, where your partner would cut them a check for the originally agreed upon amount. However, you did not tell your partner how much to pay the worker, and you find out later that your partner paid him at the higher rate than originally agreed.

What is your response to the situation?

What would accountability have you do?

How you answer the questions above will reveal how you think and what you feel is justice and accountability for the situation. Obviously you cannot control the actions of others. That is why the focus should be on the tangibles or those things that we can control and not the intangibles or what we cannot control. We need to eliminate the cloudy, so we can create clarity. This is done simply by being as specific as possible when we begin a goal and continue to refine that goal as we receive more information.

As we receive more information, we can eliminate the areas that truly are taking our focus, but do not need our time. We eliminate things such as self-doubt, self-pity, and procrastination. That is when we leave room to create self-worth, self-respect, and self-efficiency. When beginning a goal it becomes an exercise in focus. By increasing our self-esteem we will increase our ability to produce results. The exercise in focus begins and ends with our mental intelligence. This is how we think things should be or what our expectations are according to the situation.

We are conditioned at least in some manner to treat new experiences like we treated past experiences. It is human nature to view and group new experiences into categories that we are familiar with so we can deal with things quicker and more efficiently. It is a natural process that is happening in milliseconds. Communication is not only what happens when we are speaking with someone else. Communication is happening every second of every day between our brain, our body, and our spirit. The outcome of learning is the choice we make to listen, learn, and respond.

The challenge is to take a step back and see if we are looking at the situation correctly and if we have learned new information that will allow us to understand the situation better and proceed with more efficiency. This is known as conditional responses and generally takes place multiple times every hour. I know this may sound like a computer gathering data, and you are right. We are blessed with the greatest computer in existence, which is in the form of our minds. However, thinking alone is not enough.

When we take a look at the hardware of our brains, we can relate this aspect of our computer to how we have been conditioned. Often times it is referred to as nature vs. nurture. How we are mentally wired depends a lot upon how we were raised, our conditions environmentally as we went through adolescence, our friends, family dynamics, etc. Our software will depend upon the choices we make in reference to challenging the status quo, who we are, what we do, and definitely regarding accountability.

Accountability changes both nature and nurture. How we are raised does not guarantee who we choose to be. It is clear, however, that our thoughts will guarantee who we choose to be. Our progression through our goals is either inhibited or accelerated based on our level of understanding and accountability. When we seek understanding, we find the opportunities to increase accountability. As we increase in our level of accountability, we find a world that currently exists, but may be limited to our current way of thinking.

This change is not an easy change and it will not happen overnight. Any change worth making is a change that will take time. A goal is not an event; it is a process that will often need lifetime and lifestyle adjustments. As mentioned above that adjustment is how we currently look at goals and the need to make adjustments. Those adjustments are made through continued understanding of ourselves and a responsibility that if we commit ourselves to doing something, that we will follow through. Each time we do not follow through we weaken our will and confidence within ourselves to succeed. We must rewire our computer (brains) to accept the fact that we may be wrong. We should question how we feel before we rely on what we thought we knew.

Much of what goal setting is comes from habit. We are creatures of habit and thus to live a life of attainment, we must live a life of goal setting. Making goal setting a habit means that we must keep our goals in our thoughts, turn our goals into actions that will reflect keeping the goals we have set. Habits provide comfort through consistency, but goals alone will not provide happiness. Happiness comes from the incorporation of positive change for sustained growth.

Happiness is not just the opposite of sadness. Happiness is life as we know it with the elements of attitude, overcoming objections that stand in our way, and gratitude for what we currently have. Each of these elements is mental and supports the idea that we create our reality and the happiness that we currently have. Do you desire more happiness? Increase your accountability and you will find more happiness.

Goal setting takes life's challenges and experiences and brings the focus from external to internal. Goals are set by individuals, teams, organizations, communities, etc. The purpose is to take the resources available and apply them into a desired outcome. Without goals, we stumble through life waiting for life to happen. When we have goals, we effectively move through life knowing what we want and make it a reality. Knowing what we want gives us a clear understanding of how we will get there. There is no more powerful tool than knowledge. As Sir Francis Bacon stated, "Knowledge is power." I would like to add that "Application is the key."

Goal setting vs. goal attainment can cause disconnect between what we want and what we achieve. Achievement is based on performance that leads to results. One of the separating factors between goal setting and goal attainment is sacrifice. Anyone can set a goal, but those who achieve are also those who believe and sacrifice. If a person does not like something, they will not fight very hard to obtain it. We need to realize that we will face resistance. The very thing we do not like to experience can be the very thing that we need to do to get results. Like a muscle that is never used, it cannot grow without resistance. Sacrifice comfort and realize we will encounter discomfort to obtain goals.

Achievement ultimately begins and ends with our beliefs and confidence. By living an accountable life, we restore the ability within ourselves to hold ourselves responsible for what we set out to do. Responsibility can all be brought back to our core, which is the thought that turns into words, actions, and inactions. We must change our actions to meet our goals, not our goals to meet our actions. When we understand that even a thought can turn into a habit if dwelt upon long enough, I believe it helps us to control our thoughts even more.

Thoughts not only eventually work themselves into our habits and characteristics, but they even influence our confidence. I love the saying that goes "let virtue garnish thy thoughts unceasingly; then shall thy confidence wax strong in the presence of God" (Doctrine & Covenants 121:45). Pause for a moment and think about what that means to you. It provides the key to not only our further understanding, but will help us to understand that our mind is the tool for fuel. Think of a big engine that requires fuel to create movement. There is little difference for our minds in reference to our actions. The thoughts that we continually house in our minds will find their way into our words, actions, and inactions. If we want to adjust the outcome (action), we must make the adjustments to the input (thoughts).

A study performed at Harvard University in 1979 compared the earnings of students who had clear, written goals with a plan to accomplish them, students who had goals but did not write them down, and students who did not have specific goals. Obviously, the very fact that these students attended Harvard put them into a category of high performance. After 10 years this group of students was again interviewed. The 13% of students who had goals but did not have them recorded earned on average twice as much as the 84% of students who did not have specific goals. Even more surprising was that the 3% of students who had clear, written goals and had a plan for accomplishing them earned, on average, 10 times as much as the other 97% combined. (Source: What They Don't Teach You in the Harvard Business School, by Mark McCormack)

A growing problem in the world today is people who go through life searching for feeling. People want to feel something so they turn to drugs, alcohol, pornography, and other forms of quick satisfaction. Life was not meant to bring entertainment through quick fixes and events. Real joy comes from the journey of exploration, discovery, and attainment. Though the road may be rough and life will provide the refiners fire, you can obtain everything you want in life if you identify it exactly, make a plan to obtain it, and work until you obtain. By quitting, you accomplish nothing besides showing that it wasn't that important anyway.

If you are looking for a phenomenal feeling, set a goal, work to achieve it, and when you have exhausted all your resources and you have either grown, achieved your goal, or both... the feeling is like nothing else. I submit that real joy, lasting, proven joy, will come when a person finds that happiness is a heartbeat away and comes through hard work, dedication, consistency, and completion. If you get into the habit of finishing what you start, while giving your full effort every day; not only will you find joy and success; you will find accountability.

"The tragedy of life doesn't lie in not reaching your goal. The tragedy lies in having no goal to reach."

-Benjamin Mays-

Chapter 5

ACTION PLAN:

A – Accountable

C – Conscious

T – Tenacious

I – Inspiring

O – Observant

N – Nimble

P – Proficient

L – Loving

A – Audacious

N – Never Quit

Action plans are really just a step by step process with measurable benchmarks along the way. Even a thought is an action within our minds and eventually leads into a physical manifestation that started as a thought. An action plan is an accountability plan and, depending upon the seriousness we place on our thoughts, words, and actions, will depend upon the physical manifestation that others eventually see or feel. Both of the acronyms above represent individual words that potentially have a variety of meanings. Our knowledge of the words, or what we think or know the words to be, will determine how we will respond to them.

For instance the word audacious can be two things. It can mean fearlessly daring and adventurous. It can also mean arrogantly insolent or impudent. It is the same word but these meanings are quite different. Much like people will see the same event but will come away with different explanations. How is that possible when people saw the same event? This exists because we all experience the world differently. Some people feel their experiences, other see their experiences, and still others experience a combination of feeling and seeing.

Much like the meanings in this example of audacious, can we now see that even when two people have the same experience or see the same thing, there could be two different descriptions of what happened? This is largely based on perspective and how we see an event, the angle, lighting, how we feel, internal and external factors, and if there are predetermined impressions or perspectives. The conclusion is to take what we think and what we know and seek perspective by discussing this with others, seeing things from different points of view, and ultimately having a clear set of standards that we base our truth and understanding upon.

Without a plan of action, we invoke a plan of dreaming or non-performance. Dreams are the building blocks of our future; however, if we never act on the dream or plan to achieve the dream, we are left with only memories of what could have been. Similarly we find many people stuck in the category of the glory days, or the good old days, or the successes that once existed. By holding onto memories of perceived greatness, we cannot face the reality of the day and the opportunities that are currently present. Growth, development, and advancement will all require action, and effective action requires planning.

I would like to ask a question to you as a reader. To this point we have challenged the idea that we are responsible for our thoughts, our words, and our actions. However, are you responsible for your body language and the non-verbal messages that you are sending? Charles Darwin challenged the idea that there was more to human interaction. In 1872 he published The Expression of Emotions in Man and Animals, which detailed his research. From this book and other studies, Albert Mehrabian, a well-known psychologist, and Ray Birdwhistell, an anthropologist, have researched the breakdown in communication and what percentage can be attributed to body language and nonverbal communication.

If we look at the percentage in communication, we will learn that the words that we speak are responsible for the least amount of communication. Nonverbal communication and body language messages are responsible for approximately 90% of our communications. We are responsible for what our body language is portraying to those with whom we communicate. If we choose to look at the body language and compare it with the words being spoken, we can quickly place the conversation into a grouping category for further understanding.

It was mentioned in an earlier chapter that grouping is something that is happening regardless of whether we are conscious or not conscious of that process occurring. Grouping allows us to learn quickly and use our experience to make decisions to help us dissect a message. When looking at our experiences, we must research how our decisions of the past have outlined our present and will predict our future. The action plan begins by looking at what our past experiences have taught us. The first step in our action plan is to detail in our life what are the biggest factors for truth, what we consider important, and accept the fact that we are not always right. Challenging our past experiences will either strengthen our understanding that a correct decision was made, or we will find that adjustment is necessary.

When we get into the habit of objectively looking at our lives through the window of our decisions, we can find the root of our decisions which is our thoughts. Action or accountability begins with our thoughts and challenging ourselves to think on a higher plane. Challenge yourselves to be conscious of the mediocrity that surely comes on a daily basis. This also means that we avoid self-defeating talk or thought, about ourselves or others.

No matter how justified we may think we are in the criticism of others, we must remember the simple rule of not passing a judgment toward others until we have walked a mile in their shoes. Finally, we must challenge ourselves to avoid useless thoughts that take us from our responsibilities of work, school, relationships, family, and even recreation. Action begins, not only with the thoughts we have, but more appropriately with the thoughts we choose to entertain.

As mentioned before we must accept that the vehicle for greatness, attainment, and success is disguised as "change" in the form of a beat-up Chevrolet. What I mean by this is that our nature is to reject the very word, action, or application of change. We look at it as undesirable, even though it will get us where we are going and we will be just fine. We will realize that as we trust our inner instinct, as we get in the car and drive, that the look of the car did not determine what was under the hood or how reliable the car actually is.

I have had many jobs in my short 32 years. Each job has taught me about myself and others in ways that enhanced all of my life. As an entrepreneur and business owner, I currently own a handful of companies and my involvement in the day to day operations is something of a chess game. Time is a commodity that I wish I had more of. I think that most people feel that way. To accomplish writing this book, I realized that my current schedule was not going to suffice. I began waking up around 5am or earlier every morning. I also operate based on lists and calendars. Naturally I am not a planned individual, but I had to change so that I could accomplish everything that

I desired. To paraphrase Stephen R. Covey, I have learned to schedule my priorities and not prioritize my schedule.

Simply putting in my time and doing the minimum required was not a luxury or an option. I also find my responsibilities increasing with my family. Our children are aging, our community is growing, and I believe the world has never been more in need of change. We had the fortune while in the midst of this book to be kinship guardians to my 15- and 16-year-old nephews. The new challenge also brought opportunity and also heartache. My brother, father to my nephews, no longer has any desire to communicate with me or my family, which is hard to deal with. However, through it all, the opportunity opens doors for understanding, development, and growth that would not be available by just passing through life.

Throughout my life I have experienced the gut wrenching and heartache that I believe all of us have felt or will feel at some point in our lives. I have no corner on the market when it comes to vacancy at the heartbreak hotel. This is life and all of us must learn to cope. Coping we can do, but I have learned that moving forward one day at a time with focus on accountability adds perspective and assurance that great things are on the horizon. I have had to harvest the attitude that good is right around the corner and I just need to keep planting seeds of positivity. With all the potential bad that has happened in my life, the good has outweighed, outperformed, and outpaced any challenges that would cover the sunshine of each day.

The best things in life are not the flashy, the expensive, or the extravagant; they are the simple, the reliable, and the consistent. Just as we cannot fully determine the value of a car without knowing what is under the hood, we cannot determine the will or goodness of a person until we look beyond the surface and peer within their soul. Taking control of our lives does not mean that we are controlling; they are totally different. Taking control is being accountable for our outcomes by focusing on a plan, taking action with what needs to be done despite challenges, and avoiding blame, doubt, fear, and jealousy.

Being controlling is to look at something or someone as a possession and treating them with actions that are driven by doubt, fear, and jealousy. Our focus than becomes: how we look at people or things and not how we would like to control the person or thing. An accountable view is to learn and apply how we accomplish our goals through emotions and logic that we can control and an outcome where everyone wins. Accountability will also support everyone involved acting for themselves. As we live accountably we encourage and empower others to do the same. When we force or press our will on others, we eliminate accountability for the individual and create feelings of suppression and distrust.

Planning is somewhat of an acquired skill. Not everyone is automatically effective in planning out their day, week, year, and future. Most people simply do what is required of them and nothing more. We all have responsibilities placed on us, but seldomly will complete satisfaction come with just doing what is expected of us. Satisfaction will come by accomplishing the tasks and our responsibilities with effectiveness or by adding value to ourselves, to others, and the world. Adding value comes by looking at what is necessary for the day and doing it with 100% of our effort. Value also comes by taking what we desire and making a plan of action to obtain and achieve. We all have responsibilities placed on us, but seldomly will complete satisfaction come with just doing what is expected of us. However, satisfaction will come by accomplishing the tasks and our responsibilities with effectiveness or by adding value to ourselves, to others, and the world. Adding value comes by looking at what is necessary for the day and doing it with 100% of our effort. Value also comes by taking what we desire and making a plan of action to obtain and achieve.

To obtain and achieve, we need to look at excuses as feet; we all have them and they all stink. There are plenty of excuses like "I do not have time," "This event happened so I couldn't," "I'm tired," etc. We are not justified in that. However, that perception is many people's reality. So in true form of challenging what we think, let us consider the principle of time. We all have 86,400 seconds per day to use. Why is it that some use their 86k differently than others? It is because they have a plan! They know what is needed for attainment and they get to work. Additionally, the focus is not on what life gives them, but what they choose to do with life.

We must become thieves in reference to time. If we want the time, we must create it or steal it from another activity. It is no surprise that many of the top performing people don't have time for TV and are usually up before the sun is. There is so much to do in a day, we must have the attitude that, if we want it, we will plan it and make the time to accomplish it. We must schedule our priorities and not prioritize our schedules. Finally, the key to success is to properly look at yourself as if excuses did not exist. Would you live differently if something was either completed or it was not completed? There doesn't need to be a reason why something prevented completion. When we arrive at that point we live accountable.

What would life be like for you with no TV? Does that necessarily mean that there would be no enjoyment? Could you find enjoyment by replacing the time wasted with meaningful things? At one point in my life, I would say, "I'm not really into self-help and development." I laugh now because I was so small-minded but convinced myself that I had exactly what I needed and wanted in life. See, the life we live is usually exactly what we want it to be. That is a hard truth and many may not accept that, because there are always going to be the examples of the person or people who have done everything right and still they are given situations that they do not deserve. I recognize those scenarios as the statistical outliers and not the norm.

Generally, I believe that people are relatively happy with their lives and accept that truth because life is good enough. If life was really bad, I believe that a person would eventually make the efforts to change. Life is not meant to be a living hell. Doing the same thing over and over again and expecting different results is the definition of insanity. That is why the principal of change is so essential for everyone in their journey toward happiness.

Could life be great? Of course it could be. However, it likely will not just appear with our current thinking and being. We must seek different perspectives, learning, and development that will bring us to that point that we are not perfect, but that we lived great.

Greatness does not necessarily equal perfection. In fact it is quite the opposite. Greatness comes through trial, time, testing, and consistency with overcoming the odds. Perfection seems to be the point at which we all would like to get to, but let's be honest, that attainment may not come in this lifetime. Being great considers that mistakes will be made and overcome, whereas perfection is the absence of mistakes. We may think that perfection is expected from others or from ourselves. Changing our perspective is important, because the stress of being perfect will drive a person mad, where the development of greatness is a step by step process.

Chapter 6

When we begin analyzing what is happening in our minds, we must look at our very nature. We are taught from the time that we are very little the word no, and can't. It is estimated that a person hears the word "no" or some form of "no" or "don't" 248,000 times by the time they are 18 years old. Another study by UCLA estimates that, in the early years of parenting, a child may hear the word "no" 400 times per day. That is 146,000 in one year. Obviously that number may be higher for some children than others, but it is safe to hypothesize that "no" and "don't" are engrained into our minds.

What then becomes of our programming? We are programmed to think "no" and think "don't," even when we were meant to succeed, develop, and live life to the fullest. Living life is not just about replacing the bad with the good, the ugly with the beautiful; it is to live great in spite of anything that would convince us otherwise. We came to this earth not to play small, but to be brilliant, capable, wonderful, and even magnificent. A popular quote that I love talks about our potential and who we really are. Though it has been attributed to Nelson Mandela, my searching has led to the fact that Marianne Williamson is actually the original author of the quote.

"Your Playing Small Doesn't Serve The World. Our deepest fear is not that we are inadequate. Our deepest fear is that we are powerful beyond measure. It is our light, not our darkness, that most frightens us. We ask ourselves, who am I to be brilliant, gorgeous, talented and fabulous? Actually, who are you not to be? You are a child of God. Your playing small doesn't serve the world. There is nothing enlightened about shrinking so that other people won't feel insecure around you. We were born to manifest the glory of God that is within us. It's not just in some of us: it's in everyone. And as we let our light shine, we unconsciously give other people permission to do the same. As we are liberated from our own fear, our presence automatically liberates others.

-*Marianne Williamson*-

On our journey, regardless of how long we travel or whatever our pace, we must face the reality that we are and were meant for more. We are meant to have goodness, hope, and happiness. Despite what other may say, feel, or believe about us, we can come to the knowledge that we have the seeds of greatness within our being. Whether we see it or not, we are the future that our world needs. We are the future of others through relationships, guidance, mentoring, parenting, and the will to continue and complete what we started.

The start, the journey, the progression, and anything that we encounter in life becomes much more rewarding when we see that accountability is the first step that we must take. It must be our focus, so we do not get bogged down in the details, but focus on the fact that we are the right person for any task. As long as we implement accountability, we are equipped with all the resources needed to work toward success and eventually arrive at a successful outcome. Removing the negative from our life is based on progression and it will take time. The first step that each of us should take is the step of accountability. We may not be able to control it, but we know by facing it, we have the ability to overcome all things that life throws our way.

One of the most life-changing events for me happened when I was 19 years old. I served a mission for the church of Jesus Christ of Latter Day Saints. What began as a will to do what was asked of young men in the church, as well as appease my parents and fit in with my friends, eventually turned into the greatest two years of my life up to that point. I left as a selfish boy who thought mostly upon what I wanted. The mission is a volunteer service, just like everything in the church. Missionaries pay roughly $10,000 to serve their mission and teach people the gospel of Jesus Christ.

Growing up in a small rural town of probably 98% Mormons, I didn't fully comprehend what others believed and how most people live their lives. I never knew that there could be so much hostility and hate toward a religion or belief system. Serving in Oregon had its fair share of challenges. With those challenges came growth and ultimately monumental chances to advance my accountability. Within my first 4 months, I memorized and read everything that I could get my hands on. I learned best through discussions we had with people and what they believed, thought, and how they lived their lives. I saw incredible experiences change my own life and my own beliefs.

On a cold winter day in Prineville, Oregon, I approached a man and we began talking. He then started into things that I didn't have an answer to. Additionally, he began slamming the church, its values, and what I was doing. The conversation sent me deeper and deeper into a state of doubt, fear, and insecurity. It was at that point that I knew I didn't have all the answers, but should at least know something of what he was speaking about. However, I couldn't shake many of the things he said and began contemplating going home. I didn't know why I was there and surely if I couldn't answer these questions, that I had no business being a missionary.

I consulted my parents and other leaders. I spoke with companions and other church members. One advantage as a missionary is that you are completely removed from the world we all know. TV is off limits, phone calls only happen twice a year, and in many ways missionaries are left to figure things out. I can't even begin to explain the loneliness and depressive situations you deal with. Once a missionary there are many expectations, but none include going home early. I spent many early hours and sleepless nights trying to figure out what I was going to do. Upon reviewing my thoughts, meditation, and prayer, I decided to stay for me and not for anyone else. That was the turning point of my service, because I was no longer there for my parents or any expectation. I was there because I needed to be there.

That wasn't the last challenging experience and in fact I can honestly declare that I cried more times than I would like to admit. During this time is when I transformed into a man. I was accountable for what I was teaching as well as what I was thinking and feeling. At no other time in my life have I felt more tuned in to people's needs. My decision to stay was the best decision I made at that point in my life. Though I have had struggles since then, I understand the beliefs of others and respect all beliefs and ways of living. Faith in anything is admirable, and seeing people willing to share their beliefs and discuss perspective changed mine forever. Going through these trials, tribulations, and even tragedy helped me see the world in a different light and allowed me to see who I really was.

Before we can replace the negative in our lives, we must recognize the negative in our lives. It is interesting to look at a person's life and the fundamental truths that make up individuals. Again, a person's perception is their reality. Many times people are unaware that they are negative, pessimistic, or fearful. It takes a mature mind to challenge the very thoughts of who we are and what we think. Pride is a very hard thing to challenge. People do not like to be wrong, especially when it comes to admitting it to self or others.

Answer the questions below to see if you fall into the category of needing a change:

> **Do you find yourself thinking that you do not deserve to be happy?**
>
> **Is there an event/s that you feel categorize you as something less desirable?**
>
> **Do you ever call yourself stupid, dumb, or an idiot?**
>
> **Do you curse at yourself?**
>
> **Have you ever purposefully injured yourself?**
>
> **Do you avoid mirrors or reflections of yourself?**
>
> **Do you put yourself down and have a hard time accepting compliments?**
>
> **Do you avoid contact with other people? Why?**
>
> **Are you your own worst critic?**

Most of us, if not all of us can probably answer in the affirmative to the list at one point or another in our lives. Everyone will experience the occasional lows in life and hard times. However, how long do we spend in those time periods? What can be done if anything to pull a person from being down in the dumps? I submit that if we take each of the questions above and think about how we can avoid the negative and focus on consistent positivity, we can eliminate negativity.

For instance, I believe that I deserve to be happy and I believe that you should be happy too. Though life constantly challenges that truth and society would have us believe that happiness is a false hope, we are designed as human beings to have joy. Ultimately that is what we all seek. So if we seek, should we not find? The truth is that our beliefs, if believed long enough and worked for with diligence and positivity, become factual.

Happiness is not just given; it is worked for and created. We have to learn to take the experiences and expand our ability to think and to feel. As we learn and obtain knowledge, we find what makes us happy and in what ways we can experience joy. Think of life as an experiment. First of all, we do not have to experience everything to know what will make us happy and what brings sorrow. We can easily see the effects of poor decision making all around us. We can also see the effects of people who are happy and learn what it is that they will do and what they stand for.

We must also understand that one person's happiness is not necessarily our happiness. That is the joy in the journey; discovering what makes us happy. Being that we are all unique and individual, we should seek what that is and pursue it. However, regardless of the individual or the environment, happiness does not come by treating others poorly. Taking away a person's dignity and respect is not a right I believe we have. Challenge, trial, and tragedy do that all on their own. We are builders, not destroyers. We are light not darkness. So give light often and without reservation. You will see a huge difference in your life and the lives of everyone around you.

One aspect that is consistent with happiness is passion. Are you passionate about something? If so, what is it and how do you get it? I believe that we do not spend enough time pondering what we want in life or out of life. I believe that often times we have a thought and make an attempt to accomplish that thing, rather than taking the time to ponder and discover what we truly want and why. Once we make the discovery we make a plan to get there.

Let me use an earlier example that many of us can relate to. We see in the media, magazines, etc. that people who are seemingly healthy are automatically happy. Though exercise will release endorphins, which are related to happiness, it does not necessarily mean that healthy people are happy. Happiness is a decision... it is an ability. We make that decision despite anything that is happening in our lives, how we feel, and potentially the challenges and difficulties we face. If we have to make the decision each day whether we will choose happiness, we will fluctuate depending upon the situation. However, if we have made that decision and surround ourselves with people and passions, we will obtain a happiness that turns into joy.

It is interesting to study the relation between marital happiness and wealth. Finances are the number one frustration and cause of disagreement within a marriage or relationship. However, a large majority of couples report their happiest times being when they were first married and usually the poorest. There are other factors that add to the happiness, but, if a couple can be happy with little to no income, why can they not obtain happiness with more money as it comes? Is it the money, the misuse of money, or the increased responsibility and stresses that come in later years? Again, as we look at the root, money is not necessarily the seed. Is money the root of all evil? I think not, but the misuse of money can sure cause a lot of issues. That is where accountability comes into play.

I once was told by a wise man that "money is only an accelerator, if you are a jerk before you have money, when you have money you will be a bigger jerk." Why, you ask? That depends on the individual, but many times it goes back to how the person perceives money. Did they see it as a way to help and serve others? Did they view money as the root of all evil? Did they feel that money would give them power and prestige like our society depicts? It is interesting that studies show that lottery winners usually end up in the same situation they were in before winning the lottery (The National Endowment for Financial Education).

Athletes and artists who earn millions per year often times end up broke. It is not the money that is the problem, it is the misuse of money and the lifestyle that people attempt to live. The one thing that is for sure is that money does not bring happiness. Again happiness is obtained long before money or the pursuit of money is recognized. Studies have shown that people who are continually inundated with technology are more anxious and have higher levels of depression. Furthermore social comparisons leave people feeling their lives are not as full or rich as others (University of Michigan, Kross E. Verduyn, 9/14/13). The simplicity of life comes from the appreciation that we have everything we need. Happiness also comes from the knowledge that whatever the difficulty, we will overcome it.

My digression into the topic of money is to provide examples that are relatable. Let me use another. Maslow's Hierarchy of needs states that a person, before anything else, desires to have their physiological needs met (Abraham Maslow, The Theory of Human Motivation, 1943). This is the biological science of functions or functioning. Though it is not mentioned within Maslow's model, communication is one of the most basic needs for a person to function. As mentioned before, two of the most powerful desires that a human possesses are the needs to have a voice or someone who validates thoughts, feelings, and beliefs, and the feeling of acceptance, a sense of belonging, or the need for love. Even though these areas are covered in the ascending levels of safety and security, love and belonging, and self-esteem, I believe that communication and what we feed our minds is fundamental to our physiological needs.

Example 6.1:

The model projects that the physiological needs or the ones that keep a person alive are covered first. There are plenty of examples of people who have these areas covered but who without communication slowly die inside. Loneliness is a reality and communication is essential to keep our minds healthy and functioning. Though we may be living because we can breathe, have food and water, shelter, clothing, and sleep, without communication these other physiological needs eventually won't matter. If we look at the model, we can see that every aspect includes a form or forms of communication. We need to consider that each level has mental implications and physical applications. Each level supports the need for interaction and communication.

When we look at people in general, communication needs are always prevalent. How they are exhibited depends largely on the person's life and their thoughts relative to their physical hierarchy of needs. However, we can see that people gather with others who are like them or people who are in similar places in life. A basic function of mankind and even the animal and plant kingdom is to be surrounded by others. As mankind has evolved and developed, this need still exists with some interesting changes. How we communicate has changed and a growing number of people today are communicating in new ways. All the media advancements in the world, though, have not necessarily led to better communication.

Consider the instance of a relationship that is ended by an email, text, or even worse, social media. Job offers, interviews, and invitations are all declined via text. These are perhaps more convenient but lack the substanance of accountable communication. Therefore accountability decreases. Ultimately the person who has to deliver a message that may not be well-received, or that is difficult, has a choice of how to communicate. When we choose to not face these situations in person or at least by talking on the phone, we choose to avoid accountability. There is also the tendency to avoid the situation altogether, thinking that it may go away or that this is better because it avoids confrontation. Living life this way lacks maturity and avoids personal development through being accountable.

By choosing to be accountable we choose to speak with the person and face the potentially difficult situation. Furthermore, we improve communication with that person and encourage them by our example to do the same when the situation comes full circle. Facing things will also create trust among the relationship. A person may not appreciate the perspective, but they can know that we will communicate how we feel and take care of situations with respect.

Some may argue with this concept of communication. It may be said that we don't owe anything to anyone and if we don't feel like talking to someone, we don't have to. First of all that is very negative and selfish. Though that may be our initial feeling, by not facing things we digress. The science of improving is either progress or digression. Plateaus are simply the stall before the fall. It is a decision that we must make each day to rise to the challenge of the day. I believe that it is our responsibility to improve ourselves and help others do the same. By being accountable, we do just that.

Replacing the negative requires accountability. We are accountable for our thoughts, both the positive and the negative. That being true, we must **monitor, adjust, replace,** and **renew**. Negative and self-defeating talk will happen; however, we replace those thoughts with positive reinforcing thoughts that give hope, power, and promise. This may be easier said than done, but make the effort to consciously replace the negative. Once you have replaced the thought, continue by renewing those positive thoughts and feelings. When we renew our thoughts, ultimately we are creating a new lifestyle. Our new lifestyle begins with a thought and progresses through to our habits and eventually becomes our character.

The four step process of monitoring, adjusting, replacing, and renewing can apply to many things. I would like to apply it here with communication. There are many uses for these words so please feel free to add in your own. When it comes to monitoring ourselves, we begin with the monitoring of our thoughts and feelings. We are conscious of what we are feeding our brains. When we become cognizant of the thought, we need to make an adjustment. The adjustment may be in the form of our attitude, and it will surely be in the form of replacing a negative thought. Our goal here is to strive toward happiness, even though there are many things in life that compete for that.

The next step is to replace the thought with something better and more positive. The reason that this is important is because replacing requires effort and effort yields performance. Our performance eventually becomes the obtainable goal. By striving toward positive thoughts we will have positive actions, we will speak positive words, and we will eventually arrive with a happy character. You may think, "well I'm perfectly happy, why is being happy so important?" Happiness in life has many effects. Happiness relates to better health, better relationships, longevity, satisfaction, and fulfillment.

After finishing college, I took a job with Pulte Homes in Las Vegas. It was a great experience especially as the housing boom was coming to an end. Las Vegas, Nevada was one of those areas hit so hard with the drowning mortgage crisis. I had no intention of riding out the difficult days. From being a loan officer through college and from my time at Pulte, I'd learned that we as a country were in a hard situation. I called some of my friends and brothers who were selling security door to door. I asked them how they were doing with the current economic crisis and they told me to pack my bags and come to California.

Like the gold rush of old, we packed our U-Haul and headed for Fresno. Despite having the apartments fully furnished and not needing ¾ of the items packed, we settled quickly. I began knocking on doors like I had done once before as a missionary, but everything was different. I didn't have the same confidence, nor was I as skilled with the conversation. Again I hit rock bottom with the fear that I couldn't do this job. I was on day six without a sell in sight. With a supportive wife and two kids relying on me, I looked in the mirror and said "you have to figure this out." I stopped pouting and started performing.

I was up early and knocked all day long. I found myself quickly catching on and being in a position where I could help others. The accountability of the situation was not to move on and find something else. It was to finish what I started and learn a new skill. We moved three times that summer, which was not an easy task. Each time we moved we seemed to have more and more resentment toward the job and the people. Unfortunately with a commission style job and most of the pay being received on the "back end," I was left with nothing as the company filed for bankruptcy.

Since my first year in the door to door industry, through a variety of responsibilities in the six years I spent in the industry, I learned the value of listening and working with customers to create win/win scenarios. The greatest thing

I learned was persistence. I could not fail, I had responsibilities and I had a higher cause. My goal getting into the industry was to fund my business ideas. Though this stretched me thin and made things very tight through the years, I learned to pick myself off the ground and get up and work. I am accountable to my family, my customers, the company who I worked with, my companies, and my employees. Persistence and the character-building process of being accountable to others in difficult times led to tremendous growth.

We may be happy, but could we be more fulfilled? Happiness should not be looked at as only identifiable, but progression based. This is where the final step of renewing takes place. We should avoid statements like "I will be happy when or if." Rather we should have statements like "I am so happy I have _____and I look forward to obtaining _____." By showing that we recognize the happiness that is already in our lives and subconsciously planning for additional happiness, we naturally identify more happiness and it becomes a snowball effect. It is a switch in our minds of looking at what we have, with happiness and gratitude and with eagerness for additional happiness.

Happiness is obtainable by planting the seeds of what we enjoy and what we are passionate about. This comes as we seek happiness and avoid negativity because it is impossible to seek both. They are separate paths and will end up with very different outcomes. Our subconscious will flow into our conscious and eventually as we focus on the positive and the journey toward happiness, we arrive at the place where we achieve a new and better version of ourselves. As we continue to repeat this process, we find that the happiest times in life are not around the corner or down the road, but we are living them right now and that through challenge, trial, and the seemingly unfair, we are happy because we made the decision to be.

Chapter 7

Turn your focus now toward the results aspect of goals and ultimately accountability. Last chapter we talked about replacing negative thoughts. Reinforcing positive thoughts was also discussed. However, thoughts and results are two different points on the path. Remember our thoughts are the starting point, whereas our results are the eventual point that we are seeking to obtain. If we only focus on results alone, we may miss the performance of a lifetime. Performance is just as much responsible for overall success as results are. So let us begin with thought, continue with performance, and arrive with the results.

The process of reinforcement can be best understood when we break it down into steps, much like the breaking down of a goal (result) into step by step performance. The steps as I will break them down are to monitor, adjust, replace, and renew.

Example 7.1:

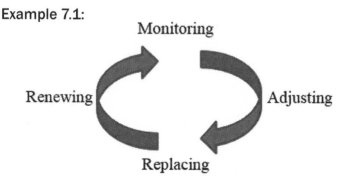

Monitoring

Renewing

Adjusting

Replacing

Monitoring – The word monitoring suggests an increased focus to someone or something. Monitoring, however, can be observing, overseeing, or overbearing. How we choose to manage usually depends on our focus, knowledge and passion. Be passionate about improvement! We have all taken on a task that has not been something we have enjoyed or completed with passion. Likely, you may have experienced something which was straining, frustrating, or even depressing. I would ask you this: Did you finish and did you give your best? How you answer those questions can give you a good idea of how you approach most things. If you can say without excuse making that you did finish or you're in the process of finishing as well as giving it your all, you can rest assured that things likely worked out with a lesson and an improved perspective.

When we attempt to observe, we either focus on the experiment or we can be comfortable with allowing life to happen. Experimenting with results, situations, or life means that we are not expecting a particular result, but we are monitoring to discover the outcome. As life happens, we observe and make adjustments as needed. Observing also means that we allow others to act for themselves and avoid making judgments and inflicting our will upon others unnecessarily. As we observe we leave ourselves open to learn and be taught by the situation and others.

Personality will define much of how we approach things and you may need to inventory how you approach things. If by nature you are more controlling, you may need to step back, breathe, and focus on the fact that the best outcome will happen. You are adequate to handle all things and by observing we will gain perspective as well as find additional options for performance. If we choose between observing, overseeing, and overbearing, we will find that observing opens us to more opportunities to develop and live accountably.

When we oversee, we are coming from a supposed higher level of authority. We delegate and try to manage the situation into an outcome that we feel to be correct. Managing rather than leading will give way to results that might work rather than allowing natural leadership to provide great success. To lead is to give people the choice to follow, whereas managing is pushing and prodding for desired results. How do you like to work? Managing ourselves is the first step along our path of progression. Many appointed managers have the immediate entitlement that what they say will go. Well hold on Bubba. Is that really the best way to get results?

All too often we feel we must constantly manage, even though the best results usually come from rolling up our sleeves and collaborating with the group for results. To be overbearing is to take the results into our own hands and control all aspects of getting something done. Consideration is not given to what others think, but manager knows best. Overbearing takes on the attitude that if you want something done, you have to do it yourself. Not true, and from an accountability standpoint, we gain no other perspective but our own. Being overbearing will also prevent the positive involvement of others and experiencing the process with a fresh set of reinforcement.

Being a father of three with another on the way has really brought this concept of control full circle. Each of our children are very different in personality and purpose. It amazes me that three little children from the same parents can be so different. I grew up in a family of seven children and my wife grew up in a family with nine children. We have experienced the differences in opinions and personalities for quite some time. It becomes different though when you are managing the welfare of another individual and you are responsible for more than their daily tasks at work.

Children are a wonderful opportunity for learning and growth. Honestly, I have never felt more inadequate for a task in my life. They will look at you with eyes that yearn for understanding and for you as a parent to step up to the challenge. At times it is daunting. With so much at stake, I began my parenting as a very controlling man. I wanted specific results and came from the school of thought that my kids would do what I say. Though that may work for some children, and certain expectations must be in place for the growth and development of the child, each of our children is so different and it is only when I look to them about how they want to be managed that I understand the best way to work with them.

Rather than expecting them just to do what I say, should I not be willing to get their input? At a time that their communication is limited, it may be necessary to implement the rules and obligations that bring consistency and balance. However, as they age, children will communicate how they want to be managed. I have learned that my children need different things and also have expectations of their own. If I go ahead and make all their decisions for them, when they leave the home they will be grossly unprepared for the tasks ahead. We must raise our children and manage others with the way they need and would like to be treated. We manage based on them eventually being able to stand on their own without our influence.

The managing of ourselves can be very similar. Some manage their thoughts similar to taking the total number of thoughts and trying to put some over here, and some over there, and oh wait we need to get these to do this. This may or may not seem familiar, but it is exhausting. What would happen if we were to take the approach of leading our thoughts rather than letting our thoughts lead us? That would mean taking what comes and allowing the things that are not important to flow toward no attention because negativity has no place in the secure, healthy, and confident mind.

The change of eliminating the negative would allow more space for the positive. Focus would be on arranging our minds to think about the items of the day that are most essential. We would stay focused because we know we are leading our thoughts and strive for development and growth. Now, what happens when those negative thoughts happen, tragedy occurs, or we make mistakes? Great, you are human, don't beat yourself up. Pick yourself up and get back on track. Remember, you can control your thoughts and that is one power that we can have no matter our circumstances.

I want to relate a story about a Holocaust survivor who spent years in concentration camps. Living on little to no food in conditions you cannot even imagine. Viktor Frankl was able to overcome all of the odds. Abuse that ranged from physical to verbal and the constant reassurance by other prisoners that they would in fact never see freedom again. As he saw his people, his race, and his religion around him dying, the natural thought might be that he would be next.

With a vision of what freedom was and the knowledge that one day he would see his loved ones again, he persisted even when that was not common, natural, or circumstantial. Viktor thought great thoughts, and even when life and time was not on his side, he persisted and reinforced the thoughts of greatness. That is the only reason Viktor eventually saw freedom and experienced the life that many around him lost. Thoughts influence everything we do, everything we say, and ultimately who we are. With that being the case, lead with the assurance that you can get out of life exactly what you want. You just need to learn how to control your thoughts, focus on positive performance, and reinforce accountable living.

Adjusting – Adjusting our behavior begins with the inventory of our thoughts and replacing defeat with journey, sadness with gratitude, and negativity with the will to achieve. Consider the example of the person walking with a rock in her shoe. Adjusting is not to simply flex her foot and move the rock to her arch so she feels it less. It is to take the time to stop, untie the shoe, take off the shoe and remove the pebble that is actually a very small piece of gold. Now this is not to think that every time we adjust we will magically find wealth untold. However, it is to give the example that when we properly make adjustments we will find hidden pieces of treasure. Treasures do manifest themselves in the form of experience, growth, and perspective which in turn creates opportunity. A great quote that gives hope:

"Opportunity is when luck and preparation meet."

-Oprah Winfrey-

Talking about adjustments is one thing. To stop and create the pattern of interruption is an action different than what we think or normally would perform. The key to adjusting is to **STOP** the action, thought, or habit. An acronym for stop that is helpful to remember is to:

S-top and consider

T-hink and reason

O-ptions for action

P-erform the best

Taking this break from the norm forces our subconscious to reconsider and possibly take a different direction less traveled. When we **STOP**, consider that for many circumstances there will be a good, better, and best option. It may not always just be good or bad. Good vs. bad is easy when we have character and implement accountability. Good vs. bad becomes increasingly difficult as we give way to justification, excuses, and victim thinking. The process of choosing good, better, or best is the journey of learning to trust ourselves and our feelings.

The best way to do this is to take an inventory of the situation, keep commitments if there are any in place, and proceed with the best option. Aligning your heart and mind is a sure way to know that you are making the right decisions. However, this does take time, life's experiences, and confidence. I refer to confidence because you must have confidence in your ability to make the right decision. Learn to lead... learn to look to yourself and your abilities to figure anything out. Remember that you were not put on the Earth to fail! Do not give your decision making away to others who may or may not know exactly how you feel and what you need.

Replacing – is action driven and dedicated to taking the negative and throwing it away. Many times in replacing, human nature is to keep the thoughts, actions, or habits close enough that we can retreat if things don't work out. Or another false idea is to never really stop the habit, by trying something with the reassuring justification that we really didn't try that hard, but we could succeed if we really wanted to. What? Replacing is not looking at things as an event, but a journey and NEW lifestyle. Our goal in replacing the negative is to develop the mental fortitude to plant the good and be willing to stay around long enough to harvest. To harvest the best in life, we must eliminate the idea that instant gratification is a way of life.

Replacing the negative or harmful requires the intelligence to put ourselves in places we can succeed and not constantly test our circumstances. Performance takes time, it takes practice. Practice doesn't necessarily make perfect... practice does however determine performance (Vince Lombardi). When we are battling thoughts, actions, or habits, would it not be safe to say that we may not be ready for battle when we are still in boot camp? Strategy takes time and it takes thought and it takes planning. We generally know our schedule so plan accordingly. We know our weaknesses so plan accordingly. If I am a man or woman who struggles with stress, our best strategy for action is to plan. If ye are prepared ye shall not fear (Doctrine & Covenants 38:30). Without a plan the anxiety of a situation becomes exponential and thus we react rather than act.

Another way to avoid the stresses of life is to incorporate the acronym of **STOP**. There are situations that are out of our immediate control. Sure, external factors do exist. However, that should not determine our actions or inactions. Fear debilitates, whereas a plan alleviates. Naturally the purpose of a plan is to prepare for unseen events or properly prepare for the known with confidence. Once we have developed the habit of planning we have understanding that will yield the experience and faith in ourselves to make the right decision even when we do not know the outcome. Success in life is tied to actions that are strategically planned and therefore success is not by accident.

Let us not wait for the outcomes, but from our thoughts, words, and actions, create the positive habits and enjoy a character that no matter the situation we reinforce the positive and eliminate the negative. Reinforcing the positive also means that we are real with ourselves, we learn to expect the best, and we are grateful for whatever will come. With anything in life, we can reinforce and experience learning, growth, and opportunity. The granddaddy of them all is choice, the choice to act or to be acted upon. How we use our agency will determine our understanding of life, freedom, and our maturity. I mention maturity because our response with anything is the composite of how we look at our involvement with life's events.

Renewing – Taking the steps that lead to renewal are the steps we have discussed with monitoring, adjusting, replacing, and then we complete the circle with renewal. Keep in mind this is not to abandon who we are, but it may mean abandoning the current defeating thoughts, actions, words, and habits. A renewal is saying goodbye to the old and embracing the NEW you. Part of being the new you is recognizing the need to always appreciate where you are because of where you have been. It also gives meaning to the reassurance that we may not be perfect but we can be great. Greatness comes based on our continual focus on the good, the better, and the best.

Don't just be good, be great because you deserve it and can obtain it (Good to Great by Jim Collins).

Renewing something is also a long term approach and not just to focus on the short term. With that in mind, let's not forget that we still must monitor the performance, or the output. The surest way for us to have this mindset of monitoring the short term and focusing on the long term renewal is to set goals. Once we have the goal, we then make the plan to perform the tasks to achieve the goal. Let's break it down. The Power of Positive Thinking by Norman Vincent Peale was a book that helped me to visualize and vocalize my goals. Do we look at our dreams as our goals or do we look at our goals as dreams? I invite you to look at your past goals and decide if you have just been dreaming. Planning is the link between dreams or goals and performance and attainment. By planning we invite the power to visualize and vocalize.

Visualization is a powerful tool and very needed to incorporate our subconscious power. Once we obtain the visual of what it is we need or want, we go to work by vocalizing it. We can start by writing it down. This is a form of vocalization because generally when we read we are saying it in our mind and this represents **Step 1**. **Step 2** is to take what we write down and position it in a place that we see often. This is an important step because we are creatures of habit and our habit for attainment has not yet been established. So seeing the reminder can quickly return our thoughts, actions, and words to our stated desires. We will gravitate toward the norm or what is comfortable so get used to being uncomfortable.

The third and final step (**Step 3**) is to make the choice to tell a select few who will hold you accountable. These are not the people that you use to "cry on their shoulder." You do not need sympathy, you need results, so make sure you get the right people. Developing accountability is not easy and it takes surrounding ourselves with the right people or seeking out these people. Holding ourselves accountable is essential, while having a support group is often the difference maker. Generally, we are so used to doing things with or for others, when we have others helping, supporting, and holding us accountable, we are more likely to get the results we desire.

Once you have the right people for support, focus on the fact that you will still need to create the direction through your goals and by holding yourself accountable. Vocalizing or step three appoints you as the conductor. Nobody else will drive your dream train, so put on your conductor hat and scream out in a loud voice: "All Aboard." Vocalize by saying your goals on a daily basis. This will make your goals more real, because this will turn goals into expectations. We are programed to take messages that we hear and implement them; that is why repetition is still the mother of all learning. You may have heard it before, but have you done it today?

Another important principle is to take the thought provided by the books The Secret (Rhonda Byrne) and The Jack Rabbit Factor (Leslie Householder). Both books are a must read and will bring great perspective. My favorite of the two, The Jack Rabbit Factor, accurately points out the work that is required along with the thoughts. To obtain goals more is required of ourselves than just making a wish list or task list. Remember you are not a task master, you are a leader. Lead your thoughts to thoughts of gratitude by vocalizing that you are grateful that you obtained the goal already. Crazy concept, perhaps, but try it before you discount it. I promise you that by saying your goals on a daily, weekly, and monthly basis, you will reinforce positive performance and get results.

Over the course of the past two years I have learned a better way to set goals and hold myself accountable. With a dry-erase marker I have written my goals on my bathroom mirror so that I see them daily. If I go out of town, I take a picture of those goals and repeat them as I am on vacation or traveling for work. The reason I did this was so I could see my goals daily. Not only can I see my goals, but naturally staring at them every morning and every night has increased my focus toward the goal, which has immensely increased my attainment of the goals.

Another trick that I have used, based on reading The Power of Positive Thinking by Dr. Norman Vincent Peale, is to vocalize those goals in the morning and in the evening. By doing this on a consistent basis I find that I am achieving my goals and am able to see daily and also nightly what needs to be done. It allows my creative mind to work freely and in the comfort and privacy of the early morning hours and as I sleep in the form of dreams. Many times I have had dreams of the very things that I am thinking about as I am asleep.

I have weekly, monthly, and yearly goals. Each weekly

goal flows into my monthly goals and my monthly goals flow into my yearly goals. There are weeks that I do not achieve everything; however, there is rarely a month that goes by that I do not obtain my goals. So far, each of my yearly goals has been met or exceeded based on making a minor adjustment. One of the largest inhibitors of reaching my goals has been that I forget about them with the daily tasks that come and go. I submit that focus and persistence is essential when seeking goal attainment.

By having your goals in a place that is visible you will continue to renew the original dream, goal, and visualization. That is powerful, because the subconscious will flow into the conscious. Our brains do not understand the difference between what we visualize and what we see. Therefore if we visualize long enough and persist through the times of difficulty, trial, weakness, temptation, or failure, we will obtain. We begin living the dream because in our mind we have already obtained it. Vocalizing is simply the next step in progression because we visualize which brings voice to our dream. Aligning the visualization and vocalization is to align our will with our power; power to perform and power to get results.

Chapter 8

It is essential that there is a clear understanding about the principal of commitment. It is impossible for lack of commitment and progress to exist together. We will either commit to something and progress, or through lack of commitment we will not progress toward our desire based on not keeping commitments. Clearly as success is sought after, we must realize that the fundamental element for progress is commitment. Whenever we perform a goal, task, commitment or when we are making adjustments, choosing progress through accountability requires commitment and it requires hard work.

Work is fundamental to progress as well, and both commitment and work equal devotion. The equation in physics for work is: Force * Distance = Work. A physics engineer named Brad Palmer explained it this way: Devotion * Commitment = Work (Brad Palmer). Devotion is another word for accountability. When devoted to something, we choose through a deep feeling, attachment, or connection to honor a decision. Devotion flows directly into commitment and commitment represents the action steps needed to comply. Work without devotion or commitment has no meaning. Simply put, our ability to achieve everything is directly connected to our devotion and commitment.

Making adjustments along the way will require challenge. The challenge will come in two forms: the actual task (and the journey toward completion), and the bigger challenge, which is to make the choice to dispute the easier way or more comfortable path. For our personal growth to occur, we must challenge ourselves to the very core of thought, action, words, and character. Challenging the thought, word or action before it is completed or taking the steps toward making the adjustments does not simply mean that a person is being indecisive or weak. Weakness comes from allowing others to complete the things that we could/should do. Weakness comes from deferring the responsibility rather than accepting and completing.

Challenging is for the strong, though decision making is a step by step process. The accountable woman or man makes a decision and does not get bogged down in extended amounts of time hoping and wondering if things will work. Strength, and therefore happiness, comes from good and bad decisions and actions. By challenging ourselves we can explore all possibilities, including the possibility that we could be wrong. We can either live our lives being right or we can live our lives being happy. By thinking we are always right, we will never know and will surely miss opportunities to learn and grow. Challenging ourselves does not mean we always arrogantly choose correctly. It does mean that we take the more difficult path, the higher road, and become problem solvers to life's difficulties.

Consider the journey of a diamond that begins as a piece

of coal. Coal begins as a natural material formed from fossilized pre-historic plant remains. Through time, intense pressure, and adversity, a piece of coal can become a tough, obstacle defying, beautiful diamond. Similarly, as individuals, though we begin as an average composite of creation and the world around us, as we experience adversity, through time and intense pressure, the average can become the accountable. Through weakness, loss, tragedy, terror, bad habits, and anything else the world will throw at you; we can become like a diamond which is a highly refractive crystalline used to cut through stone, glass, and even concrete. Be the diamond and not the cubic zirconium. The decision lies with the power to choose greatness by applying principles.

An experience that refined me, so to speak, came when we had just moved as a young family to Boise, Idaho. I was attending Boise State to get a Bachelor's Degree in Management. Within a very short time frame, we had two car wrecks, not serious thank goodness. We experienced flooding in our 2nd story apartment that also flooded the basement apartment. Additionally I had taken on a side project of completing construction on a building along with trying to take 18 credit hours. My transfer from the school where I obtained my Associate's Degree proved challenging as I lost 15 credits.

What was I to do? The only income that we had as a family was tied to a job that the senior loan officer decided he didn't need anymore. We got to work. My wife had finished Cosmetology School and began cutting hair. I interviewed to be a loan officer and was hired. Unfortunately I had to spend less time at school during this time and ended up having to drop my calculus class as well as struggling in other classes. We finished the building, but did not make anything worth writing home about. Everyone was paid. Despite the lack of effort from some of those we hired, it all worked out. If not for Roger, the building owner and consequently the mortgage broker and my direct boss, we would not have been able to pay everyone.

It was an expensive lesson and I learned my limits for stacking too many things on my plate. Without a good wife who was willing to go to work and a great family who was willing to watch our little girl, we simply wouldn't have made it. I remember my wife taking lunch breaks and other breaks just to feed our baby and still be able to work. We wouldn't have made it without her effort. We also wouldn't have made it without a clear commitment to each other and to our future. When trials arise, it is important to know that you can make it. What is required is the decision you make before the trial comes, and the courage to make it through the trial with support for everyone involved.

The difference between try and triumph is the umph. Get in and give it all you've got. There is no reason to slack or just try. Give everything you have and more will be provided. When we get into the habit of giving our all, rather than giving excuses, we are quickened. We are given additional umph to succeed and exceed our own or others' expectations. This quickening comes through confidence. We will trust ourselves in giving our all and through giving our all, we will be provided with additional opportunities and learning that come through taking on tasks, projects, and life with our full focus and effort.

Opportunities are the additional thoughts that come through the experience. Remember to learn from the experience and to experience the learning. Opportunities will include the physical manifestations that come from our subconscious creation and the natural flow of work into our conscious. Opportunities will finally come in the form of increased awareness that our confidence is growing and we are developing. This process of recognizing opportunity and taking action is built around eliminating the mediocre. Mediocrity is a contagious disease. It weakens mankind and the desire for progress and opportunity. Identify it in your own life and immediately get it out of your life.

The goal to become a better version of ourselves requires an acute awareness of the world around us, the opportunities, the people, and the progress. Learning comes from all sources and as we develop the habit of learning from others, we consider all things within our lives as a teachable quest. We learn because we choose, not because we experience alone. We cannot count mere experience for the learning of something completely, until we consider the application and choose to challenge or adjust our current way of doing, living, and being.

Experience ➔ Learning ➔ Growth ➔ Development ➔ Disposition

Who we are depends upon our experiences. As we have mentioned throughout the book, we must understand that experience alone will give us a sense of feeling or possibly further knowledge on a subject. However, experiences should not lead to feelings of entitlement or the arrogance of being an expert. There are many factors to consider when looking at the overall situation. Being an expert comes from experiencing something over time or multiple times and defining the best course for self and others. Accountability provides the mental discipline, maturity, fortitude, and physical and mental strength to see the situation from many different viewpoints.

When we consider all the factors that affect others, and choose to be accountable for the situation and possible outcomes, we have chosen to progress rather than remain. To remain is to forgo growth and opportunity. Choosing to be accountable will also include sacrifice. We sacrifice the insatiable need to be right, to prove others wrong, and the feeling of our manufactured comfort zone. Sacrifice is largely tied to accountability and the progress of a person. We choose to build a foundation of consideration for others, ourselves, and the world rather than manufacture a comfort zone built for one.

The pages of our lives are often written in adversity. Adversity in life will often create perspective and our disposition. As we continue through life and experience times of learning, growth, success, failure, and adversity we will choose how we will respond and therefore move forward or stay the same. Disposition, much like character, begins with a thought and will eventually imprint upon our faces as our look, our demeanor, and our body language.

With communication as it is, our disposition is the composite of meta verbal, Para verbal, and body language factors. Disposition is determined by knowledge, education, experience, understanding, and accountability. Accountability is the crowning characteristic to all the other determining factors. As such, accountability provides advancement in knowledge, education, experience, and understanding. When we choose accountability, we choose greatness in the face of excuses, misunderstandings, victim minded thinking, and fear itself. Remember, what you focus on most is what will eventually find its way to the surface of what others see.

Exercise 8.1:

Imagine you are a person who is high-flying in your career. Your ideas are great, people listen to you, and you seemingly can do no wrong. As you venture out one evening with work associates, tonight seems different and you have the thought to stay in and rest. However, in the spirit of fun, you decide against your better judgment. As you enjoy the evening you are realizing that the later it gets the less ambition you have. You find yourself in a conversation about the boss's family and everyone is taking shots and criticizing. This represents your first opportunity to choose accountability. What do you do?

Conversations continue, and volume increases. Over time, you are asked your opinion. This is your second opportunity to choose accountability. You stay mostly diplomatic, but do make some points that others laugh about and join. Things begin getting out of hand and it mostly revolves around your comment. This represents your third opportunity to be accountable. What do you do? The conversation gets so off-color and inappropriate that people who are not with your group begin making faces of disgust. As others in the group notice onlookers, one boisterous man in your group begins cursing at other patrons. This represents your fourth opportunity to be accountable. What do you do?

The next morning you wake up one hour late and now consequently you are late for work. This represents your fifth opportunity to be accountable. What do you do? You arrive at work to find a meeting has already happened and the boss would like to see you in his office. As you arrive in his office, there is another individual in the office, who you learn is your boss's sister. She identifies you as a participant in the group and even mentions that you were one of the main contributors. This is your sixth and final opportunity to live accountable. What do you do?

Though this is just an example, this does happen. Perhaps not as dramatically; however, there were points along the way where adjustments were needed. Those adjustments were and are accountability. Accountability teaches us that we should not speak of others when they are not there to defend themselves. This does not mean that we cannot be real and confront a person with issues, challenges, and frustrations. This should be done in private. It is very simple, but it will serve you in all your relationships. Accountability provides understanding that we assume the best in people and hope for the best in situations.

This situation happens every night in every community all over the world. Rather than gathering together to enjoy time with other employees, as late evenings often do, ambitions often shrink. Be the strength so others feel like you are not going to join the conversation just to be a part of the group. Be the example so that others know they have an ally when and if they are not part of the next gathering. Choose to influence the conversation without coming across as being so much better than they are. However, make it clear that you will not participate in a roasting of someone who is not there, or even if they are there, you will not take from their personal dignity or respect. Accountability requires more than "everyone is doing it."

One of the best quotes that apply to the exercise above, as well as all areas of life, states that:

"Great minds discuss ideas; average minds discuss events; small minds discuss people."

- Eleanor Roosevelt-

Having read her biography, I can tell you that she endured heartache, suppression, discouragement, and adversity after adversity. With adversity there is a choice. Through accountability comes greatness. We all can thank Eleanor Roosevelt for her tireless work with women's rights, equality, human rights, and making the world we live in a much better place. She stood for accountability in all of her actions toward the poor, she stood against racial discrimination, and she drafted one of the greatest works, known as the Universal Declaration of Human Rights (www.un.org/en/documents/udhr). Because of her work and her life, we all benefit. May we all live with the same desire to create and make the necessary adjustments for an accountable world.

Chapter 9

Accountability is brilliance! Why would the will to take responsibility be brilliant? The definition of brilliant is: full of light or shining brightly. Bright and vivid in color as well as glorious and magnificent are also associated. Accountability creates within individuals the ability to repel fear and move forward with action. Accountability is actionable and based on making decisions and movements in a positive direction that will bring results. I choose the word brilliance because accountability is becoming a lost art. Fewer people are found with the ability to take on the challenge of being great by choice. Even when facing similar trials as everyone else, a difference in attitude and power comes through being accountable.

The great news is that all of us have the seeds of greatness within us. Anyone can be great and many people have flashes of greatness thrust upon them. Brilliance comes from the constant quest of being our best self through accountability and bringing others with us for the journey. As we realize that life is the composite of human experience, development, and understanding through perspective, we begin to learn that we can judge our success based on the influence we have on others. People are searching for that guiding light of perspective. Accountability creates a niche for characteristics that people want to be around. That guiding brilliant light shows through our thoughts, our words, our actions, and our character.

Focus for a moment on those who have given you the perspective that you currently have. It may be parents, grandparents, community members, friends, spouse, etc. Likely your perspective comes from the accumulation of these relationships, experiences, and knowledge. A natural draw for mankind is to seek others who are like us or support us, or even make us feel better. With all of life's challenges, it becomes essential to have these relationships and seek people who add to our lives and not take away.

It is like the analogy of a bank account. We should seek those relationships that credit our account and avoid costly debits. Debits over time, with no credits, leads to difficulty in finances and has additional effects that flow into our psychological and mental health. Money is something tangible that we can all relate to. However, do we not see the same importance or place the same focus on the seemingly intangible? Relationship health and communication are a focal point toward our overall health and well-being. More focus should be placed on balance in our heart and mind. As we align both the heart and mind, we are not only more at peace, but we have better confidence, and the light in our lives is noticeable.

I would like to share a story of someone who was brilliant in my life. Not only was she very intelligent when it came to school work, but her last act embodied her light or brilliance for others. My sister Lisa Marie Schwab passed away May 11, 2013, at the age of 35. Her passing was due to a massive seizure that was sudden and brought with it reflection and new perspective. I didn't get to say goodbye or tell her I loved her. In fact, her last text, I didn't even respond to. Because of her brightness, she was also troubled throughout her life with darkness, often times those who are the brightest have to fight the darkest nights.

Lisa battled depression, hurt, loneliness, and despair. She ventured into a world of addiction and with it came many other effects. It was difficult to have her around because she was not herself and clearly her lifestyle did not support her long term goals. There was a point where as an individual I was pushing all interactions away based on lack of understanding and the perceived protection of my family. However, when she needed me most, I was not there. She needed love and not criticism. I remember poking fun and joking about her behind her back and saying things that now only fill me with regret. Her loss has been felt in the homes of her family and friends everywhere.

She was always my protector, and there was more than one time when she stood up for me and acted in part to keep me from harm. I only wish that I would have done the same for her in her time of need. She lived for having fun, but also lived to help others, especially the weak or picked on. Her example in life has simply changed my perspective and will to be accountable no matter what. Her goal was always to be an organ donor. I am happy to report that she did in fact reach that goal. Her heart and lungs went to recipients to provide life for two people in

California. Her pancreas and liver went to two individuals in Arizona who now can live an improved life.

This experience brought hurt and pain, but a new challenge to live great and become the person she saw me as. She believed in me and always was so supportive of all my dreams. She is a large part of my life and I continually have experiences, hear songs, and have fond memories that remind me of how much she did for me and the world. My desire is to live with the same brilliance Lisa did daily in the form of hope and service for those in need. To my sister Lisa, I want to thank you for being my protector while you were on this earth and I have no doubt that your influence will continue on the other side.

Our brilliance shows through our demeanor. It does not matter how successful we may be or accolades that we obtain. Brilliance is not about money, power, or prestige. Brilliance is about light and the spreading of brightness to others. The way that we bring the light to others is we choose to live accountably. Living accountably includes the standard of doing to others as you would have done to you. Accountability focuses not on self, but through self we serve others. We realize that we are a source for positive change and reinforcement for people's lives. How can that be? When we look at the words most closely associated with accountability we discover; honesty, focus, confidence, responsibility, and willpower.

I would like to speak about each of these traits not so much as what they are, but what they mean and how they can be applied. These traits are heavily influenced by our perception, psychology, and the environment that is our reality. Some may argue that these traits are subjective in nature, but I would like to establish consistency relative to accountability.

Honesty is many things and can have many applications. However, honesty within the framework of accountability is to first evaluate self. Honesty starts with each of us and causes us to look at our thoughts, actions, and words by evaluating consistency, intent, and morals. It should never matter who is present or who is not present. Honest accountability does not change by the environment, the crowd, or the situation. That is why it is so essential to make a decision before we are encountering the option. When faced with split second decisions, heightened emotions, and peer pressure, if we have determined our standards before those moments of decision, we will make consistent and calculated choices based on what is really important.

Most people know the difference between honesty and dishonesty, but we can also look at good, better, and best decisions in which all three options represent honesty. One decision will clearly be better than the others. One question to ponder: Does honesty always represent proper ethics? What is acceptable may not always be honest and that is why both must be considered.

Let me provide an example. My daughter was vacuuming our car the other day. I was using the shop vacuum and my daughter came to me initially and said she could not vacuum the car because the home vacuum's hose was not long enough.

I asked her if there was another option she had not considered. She said there were no other options. I told her that it might take longer, but she could get another extension cord and wheel the vacuum to each car door so that it could reach. She then came back to me, telling me she could not vacuum the trunk area because there were things in the way. Honest? Yes, there were things in the way. Ethical? No, she knew that our standard for vacuuming the car was to do the entire vehicle and that would mean moving things that may already be there.

Though this is a simple example, we see evidences of this throughout society. We see this often times in the work force, in that an honest day's work has different meanings depending upon who you ask. Simply showing up for the day does not necessarily mean you put in an honest day's work. Ethics raises the bar by completing tasks honestly, but also doing the task with full effort and attention. The personal application in regards to goal setting and goal completing is that we can "just" finish a task, or we can complete it with 100% of our effort. As we exert more of ourselves according to our standard of ethics, we learn more and we become more. Happiness is increased as we focus not only on completion, but completion to our best abilities.

The biggest realization to recognize is that justification and accountability do not exist together. Justification leads to excuses and excuses will lead to habits. Because excuses are created to protect, create a white lie, or lessen responsibility, they are used as a defense mechanism to eliminate the feeling of discomfort. Excuses also represent some form of fear toward responsibility or the capacity to deal with the situation. The tendency is to take the easier route because the commitment has not been made. By eliminating excuse making, we choose the path of acceptance and responsibility, which naturally brings accountability.

Do not let society define your ethics or your happiness. Happiness and accountability are entirely up to you. At any age, regardless of our external circumstances, our thoughts will determine our state of mind and therefore our happiness. Furthermore, our happiness in life leads to the brilliance (brightness) of our external circumstances. That is why society, the world, or anyone else should not determine your personal ethics or happiness. This is the quest of a lifetime, to find happiness and live that happiness daily.

Focus is both conscious and subconscious. Every time we have a conscious thought, we have changed our subconscious platform. As our subconscious flows into our conscious, our thoughts are manifested into a physical form. What then should we focus on? Focus is not only what we choose to think about, it is diverting our energy away from the negative and making a choice to the positive. Consistency in turning to the positive eventually brings success through renewed focus, increased energy, and success. The success I mention is the success that comes by winning the battle in the mind. This is where it all begins. This is where greatness or weakness, like a well of water, springs forth into action. By overcoming ourselves through thought control, we are empowered to overcome other obstacles.

Whether you recognize this or not, you are in training. We all are in training. Much like an athlete who trains their muscles to prepare for an event, or a season, or success in their given field, we train to overcome our minds. When the feeling of defeat comes in our life, where did that begin? Making the choice toward focus is making the decision to direct our thoughts into feelings. Though we may feel physical pain or experience injustice, how we focus on overcoming those feelings through our thoughts will tell the story of our personal strength, our fortitude, and our confidence. This process cannot be given justice through words alone. It is an experience that all must face and overcome. Let me be clear in that weakness is not a one-time event or decision. Weakness, like strength, is built over time and through consistent focus.

I like the word focus because it is a word that lends to the power that each of us has to influence our thoughts. Concentrate for a moment on the word focus and what is required for a higher level of performance. While focus alone is good, we can do better. When we visualize the result or choose through our focus to visualize the day, our tasks, situations, difficulties, and how we will respond, we choose brilliance. The brilliance or brightness creates in our subconscious the power to move and become. Our minds do not know the difference between what we see physically and what we create subconsciously through visualization. That is why there is such great power in visualizing our success on a daily basis. Remember, success is not a random event. It is planned and calculated through our focus.

Focus is not just an increase in attention to something, focus is follow-through toward completion. We are not merely visualizing something as it is, but as it could be. Much like the focus that we put on things, we can similarly put a focus on ourselves; not what or who we are, but who we can become. Focus, like accountability, is about action and follow-through. As we learn brilliance through accountability, we realize that we do not simply speak to be heard or announce that we will be doing this or that. Our actions will always speak louder than our words and therefore should dictate our focus. Don't just be a talker, because as they say talk is cheap. Be a doer.

Confidence is the aspect in our life that brings assurance. Rather than thinking of confidence from the perspective of whether a person has it or doesn't have it, let's ponder the uses and benefits of confidence. Whether we know it or not, every action performed is done with confidence or the lack thereof. It is part of our make-up, our spirit, and what helps a person to make decisions and follow through. Brilliance, as we know, is about commitment and follow through, but will also include the "how" of confidence. Confidence is not the absence of fear; it is to know a situation, ourselves, and to take courage. All we need for achieving anything is all around us.

Think for a moment about an example that I would like to provide. If today you were asked to start writing a book about your favorite subject, could you do it? Now, what was the first thought that you had at that very moment? Your mind just went through a quick reasoning of the task and whether you could perform that task. However, our confidence is wired into our subconscious. We will either have the certainty or positivity to take on the task based on our ability to conceptualize. That is where our confidence or the lack of confidence first exists. Similar to accountability, the confidence a person has begins within their thoughts.

Could this progression not just be about accountability and confidence? This is a principal of life and of living. Everything begins at the micro level of a thought and continues through to our actions and inactions. As we are creatures of habit, or comfort, our actions will turn into habits and our habits find their way into our characteristics. Brilliance is the same and you will start identifying the principal in other areas. If we are to influence the action, we must influence the thought. When we look at the thought we must consider the confidence.

Confidence is something that you cannot just tell a person, "Hey you why don't you just have confidence, it is that easy." Having or more accurately exhibiting confidence comes from how we view ourselves in relation to the world, our peers, and the elements of life that surround us daily. Confidence does not have to be a comparison game, and we do not make great progress when we compare ourselves to others. We only see the outward actions of a person who we may think has it all, or is perfect and surely does not deal with what we do.

That thought alone is false and a defeating strand of thoughts will continue so STOP! Even though people may be put together on the exterior and everything may look like it is going great, I believe that each of us would be shocked if we could learn what burdens people carry. Life has a never ending supply of lemons, so it would be wise to learn how to squeeze the best from them for lemonade. Each lemon, just like each of life's experiences, is different and unique. Furthermore, with the discovery that each lemon can be squeezed or life's experiences overcome, we can become efficient regardless of the challenge.

I heard of an exercise that would be good to mention here. A group of ladies sat in a room and spoke about some of the difficulties and challenges that each was facing, and how to continue to have the strength, faith, or what I will refer to as confidence to press forward. Each woman wrote on a piece of paper the challenge that they were dealing with or had dealt with in the past and folded the paper and put it in a bowl and passed it around. Once everyone had participated the bowl was passed to the front, where these challenges were read to the group. After hearing what others were going through and some of the difficulties faced, the general consensus was that each person would have preferred to keep their own challenges.

We will never know completely what others are dealing with because we do not know their thoughts. We can feel confident in the fact that the things that we deal with and will deal with are for us and that there is a reason that we are dealing with them. I believe the reason we deal with challenge is to obtain growth and progression, which is provided to us by our loving Deity. Whether or not that is a personal belief that you share, I can tell you with complete confidence that you are much more valuable than you allow yourself to believe. In many ways we become conditioned to expect the worst or think that bad things will surely come. Over time, we become aware of that message and as a defense mechanism to protect ourselves, we often choose to remain rather than create.

Each of us can remember a time in our lives that we were confident. It may have been when we were children, or youth, or in college, or perhaps our most confident years were in our 20s, 30s, etc. Why? Was it because we looked a certain way? Was it due to the people we had in our life who validated who we were? Whatever the reason, confidence should not be dictated by how we look, but more about what we feel. That feeling of confidence or performance is what has been missing. Confidence brings happiness. I assure you, that if you can look into your life and ponder why that time was different, you can make the adjustments to seek that feeling again. Life happens, and tough things are distributed to everyone, but let us not get wrapped up in the past, but create the exact future we want.

Creating what we want is difficult, but not impossible. There will be things that you will need to stop doing. There will be other things that you will have to do. One thing is for sure, though; you will need to change the way you think. Think of yourself as a powerful, confident, and courageous person who can do anything that is placed in your path. You may not be there yet, and even being at that point doesn't mean you will be free from mistakes and blunders. It does mean, though, that through the mistakes, you will be quickened and receive the light you need to be the best version of yourself. Remember that comparing yourself to others will only leave you with a feeling of insecurity. Compare yourself to yesterday. Are you doing better? How about last month or last year? Progression, like confidence, will take time, attention, and courage.

Responsibility is a debatable trait that has conflicting views. Some think that their only responsibility is for themselves. Selfish, perhaps, but we also don't know why a person may think that way. Let's look at what makes up who we are: we are a citizen, a child to someone, an employer/employee, a pet owner, a tenant/owner, a friend, a confidant, etc. Perhaps we are a sister, a brother, a parent, a soldier, another person's happiness, a future. The truth is, we may not know what we are to others. Our meaning goes beyond how we view ourselves. Our meaning is often defined through the responsibility that we choose to accept and how others look to us.

We can know one thing for sure; we are a servant. What do I mean by that? Your first thought may have been, "no I am not." I am a free man or woman or I am this or that. My definition of servant is perhaps different than you may expect. I look at servant as responsibility or the will to take care of our duties or ultimately to be accountable. We are accountable to our thoughts, words, actions, etc., but are we not also accountable for what we have and what we have been given? Gratitude is often associated with how a person views what they have or what they have been given, but it also is a way of life. Are we grateful for each day? Do we show gratitude for the people, our minds, our bodies, our perspective? We all have much to be grateful for.

By living a life of gratitude, we change our focus and therefore the outcome. Gratitude is not just an attitude, it is a way of thinking, being, and becoming. Studies have shown that those who exhibit a life of gratitude have less stress and have a higher satisfaction out of life (www. greatergood.berkeley.edu, Gratitude and well-being: A review and theoretical integration, by Alex M. Wood, Jeffery J. Froh, and Adam W.A. Geraghty). Truly, we could be grateful for something every day and begin a journey to see how many things each day that we might find that we could be grateful for. I fully recognize the difficulties that arise from loss of job, loss of loved ones, difficulties with loved ones, strained relationships, and poor decisions. If we live bogged down by the decisions we have made, we will always be floating, with just a big wave between surviving and drowning.

One concept that accountability supports is the idea of forgiveness. It also begins with each of us and is validated and seasoned based on our own efforts to forgive the poor decisions we have personally made. This way of doing becomes a way of living as we extend the same service to others. Like ourselves, nobody is perfect, and we can learn to forgive others because we choose to live accountably and not blame others. When someone wrongs us, it becomes easy to blame, and hate, to criticize and even ostracize others. Are there actions that are unpardonable? Perhaps, but that is something that you must decide for yourself. I believe over time even the most challenging of actions or choices can be forgiven.

Recently I was given a situation that shed light on something that I did not know and could not comprehend. Someone who I love and respect very much had made a decision years before, which was not supported by the way they lived their lives or told me how to live mine. When I discussed this event with the person, excuses and blaming were brought up. Eventually, the individual asked that we leave it in the past. After much thought, I have come to conclude that the event happened, but it is not happening. There were steps taken to eliminate the unhealthy actions from their life. I was not informed at the time of its happening because it was not my business, nor would it have brought goodness or further understanding into my life.

Ultimately the individual is bright, and resilient, and over time they have made necessary changes. Though I still am in need of time and further understanding to process the whole situation, truly the event is in the past and does not represent the present nor the future. Forgiveness for me was to look at not only what the situation was and how it affects my life now, but it also represents a lot of the ways that I think about myself, others, and how I view my relationships. It has been hard, because at the heart of the situation, I find that trust is the thing that has been challenged the most. However, in knowing the individual and not necessarily the decision, I find peace knowing that I am in need of forgiveness too.

This new perspective has given me power to overcome

the thoughts that sneak their way into our minds of defeat, cynicism, doubt, hate, and fear. There are plenty of thoughts that will come, that we may or may not want to live up to. Accountability would have us look at these thoughts, maturely categorize them, and move forward with responsibility or the ability to respond positively. Responsibility, as I have learned, is the ability to respond and not necessarily the form that we understand to be task oriented or answer based (Robert Duncan). Viewing responsibility this way allows us to appropriately process our intent positively and avoid the pitfalls of negativity.

Willpower is the final aspect to brilliance through accountability. Perhaps most importantly, we find from within the true desires of the heart. We have seen examples of the will to live and a willingness to understand or even the experiences of people willingly taking something upon themselves. Whether we choose it ourselves or it is thrust upon us, we will all have the chance to achieve greatness; and if not greatness why not brilliance? The brightness explained from within, by the definition of brilliance, is no more influenced than by the power to choose or our willpower.

We must understand at this point that we made the choices that have led us to today. We must understand that by those choices we have joy and also unfortunately some pain and discomfort. Though you may not have specifically chosen the external challenges you've experienced, by choosing your next move, you did choose your response, your mental state of dealing with the challenge, and you chose your future. By design, we are given full power to be the captain of our sea. Everyone wants to drive the boat when the weather is nice and when cruising with friends. However, who takes the helm when the storms of life arise? When there are waves crashing down on you and the ship is about to sink, who then takes the wheel? And after the storm when the calm comes, as it always does, who then will make the necessary repairs to the ship?

I submit to you that it is your willpower! It may not always be you making the repairs or taking command of the ship. It is, however, the will by you or someone who cares about you to help steer the ship to safety and then make the necessary repairs. When a person is drowning, often times the mind focuses only on that struggle and fails to recognize opportunities for safety, and the instruction to remain calm, to relax, and to swim. Life will not be played primarily in the kiddie pool where we may tower above the dangers of drowning. Life gives you an ocean to swim in and then provides storms, hurricanes, and even tsunamis to test our will.

I am not suggesting that everything will be adversarial in life, unless we choose to think in that way. However, I am suggesting that with the tests in life, there is calm that follows. There is safety from the storms of life, but safety requires recognition of where safety can be found. It requires the willpower to get to that safe place. There is always deliverance given by the will to succeed, the will to change, and the power to will or willpower. Explore and then discover the willpower within you and how you can benefit from knowing who you are, what you want in life, and working your hardest for the things which you believe will make you happy. If happiness is the key, be prepared to work for it, and as times, seasons, and maturity change, be prepared to change or pivot toward what is best.

I have a very close friend who has a very serious addiction. I have consulted my friend many times about the addiction and how he may overcome the problem. Let me first be clear that addiction is the most misunderstood disease. I submit that disease begins as perception and progresses through the seemingly logical to the illogical. First of all, an addict does not feel like they have a problem. They live in a state of denial and create the world around them that supports their behavior. Secondly, they think they have a deep well of self-control that they can draw from and push the limits where everything will be just fine. Thirdly, whether they can admit it or not, the very root of the struggle is willpower. Willpower is the source from where they will learn to rebuild, build, and remodel.

Conversely, addiction looks at life selfishly and from the rose-colored glasses of "I have to have" and "I can't help myself." Really? Well then, can we not be addicted to doing the right things? Can we not be addicted to being true and honorable? Substance abuse introduces chemicals into the brain and body that make this more difficult, but not impossible. My friend, who I will refer to as Tuck, has a very serious addiction to pornography. Unfortunately, Tuck is not alone in this addiction or other addictions. There is enough evidence in the world around us that addictions are destroying people, they are destroying families, and they are destroying society.

Addiction alters the state of mind, but it is not only in the brain; addiction extends to the body as well. No more is the pattern from thought to character more obvious than in the life of an addict. They do not choose to have the willpower over their thoughts. As they think about their addiction enough, they begin to act to get their fix. This comes in the forms of lying, belligerence, force, and deceit, but it does end in an action. This action and the words, specifically the self-talk and justification within the mind, will lead to a habit. Once a habit, it is only a matter of time until it is a person's character or in this sense the addiction.

We do not have to accept addiction as though we are powerless to change or make a difference. Though there are evidences that addiction will eventually eliminate willpower, there are also constant reminders that there is help and support (Donald L. Hilton). Often times a person must hit "rock bottom" to realize that change is desperately needed. No addiction is more powerful than a person's will to overcome, albeit with the support of a group and the necessary support that comes through trained professionals. That is unless the person does not have the willpower to change. Without willpower, neither the addict nor mankind will achieve freedom from challenge, freedom from oppression, and freedom from life's difficulties.

There is a reason that support groups meet often and speak openly about their challenges. There is also a deeper purpose behind these groups which comes in the form of recognition and acceptance. Recognition comes in the form of knowing that the attendees are addicted. The first step of recognition is to admit there is a problem/addiction. The related action is to recognize that you have a group who understands and that you can relate with. The other form of recognition is to accept that there is a higher power and one that can deliver the addicted from the addiction.

I would ask you now to digress in your mind as to how this may be applied in your life. Do you have any addictions? If so, what are you doing to overcome the addiction? What are some of the results if the addiction is continued? I recommend that you seek the help needed to recognize that you are not alone and that help is all around you. Sadly, it may not always be in the form of understanding from others. It may not even include your family, but it will include the recognition that there is a higher power and you are endowed with the willpower needed to obtain freedom.

Freedom is to happiness as willpower is to brilliance. The person with willpower reflects a life of accountability, which is brilliance of life and provides a brightness of hope. The challenges of today are more difficult than they were yesterday. Never fear, because the test of today is preparing you for the performance of tomorrow. In reality our willpower is affected by the environment in which we live. However, at the end of the day it comes down to the choice to think, the choice to reason, and the will to live great.

We have the ability to choose our thoughts, words, actions and inactions, but we do not get the luxury of choosing consequences. The brilliance of accountability is that we make decisions knowing that whatever the consequences, we are responsible and committed to accepting whatever happens as our responsibility alone. No other factor either external or internal can take the blame, we cannot make an excuse, it was not anyone else's fault, and no, not everything bad always happens to you. A victim minded approach keeps us locked in the past where excuses run wild. An accountable life provides the details, the clear picture, and the focus for our present and our future.

Here is a quote that embodies the very brilliance of accountability. If we apply these suggestions, we will have success, love, and happiness despite the challenges we encounter.

Words of Wisdom

Approach each day with positive thoughts.

Believe in the goodness of others.

Create a better world by being a friend.

Decorate your life with beautiful things.

Educate yourself through the teaching of others.

Find friendship through the giving of yourself.

Gain insight into others by being a good listener.

Hope will keep dreams alive.

Imagination is the key to success.

Judge no one but yourself.

Keep yourself focused on your goals.

Live life to its fullest.

Make happiness your primary goal.

Nothing can stand in your way when you dare to dream.

Open your eyes to the world around you.

Persevere when it seems impossible.

Quality of life comes from doing the things you enjoy.

Respect the values of others.

Strive to do your best in all things.

Take hold of your own destiny.

Unity of mind and soul makes for inner peace.

Value the little things.

Welcome input from others.

Explore new opportunities at every chance.

You live your life, others will live theirs.

Zest for life will help you live at your peak.

-Author Unknown-

Learning comes from observation, knowledge comes from application, and wisdom comes from experience. If we can learn how to take these suggestions and implement them into our lives, we will obtain brilliance. Brilliance will bring brightness, vividness in color, and/or character that is shining brightly as well as gloriously. Though brilliance takes time, energy and effort; the work provides a unique and magnificent way of living that brings accountability and opportunities that change the world.

Addendum #1

Addiction

Addiction is the most misunderstood disease! However, if we never start something, we never have to stop. Where we don't completely understand addiction, we should not entertain things that are not good nor provide us with long term happiness. It comes down to having a set of standards and morals and making a choice once. It is understood that willpower is largely effective in avoiding addictive habits or substances (Donald L. Hilton). However, there is a time where willpower is no longer part of the equation. Discipline is mandatory in helping a person provide consistency in life. Furthermore, a person loses the power to choose and the discipline to become, through addiction. The reason being is that our desires and perceptions change to reflect the addiction. The truth is that when we start an action, we do not necessarily know whether it will be an addiction.

Addiction will get a person to the point of planning and committing all of their time, focus, and energy to obtaining the habit or substance. Allow your willpower to be a powerful force and for your choices to matter. When you're addicted, your choices don't matter, and you will have lost the will to choose. Addiction will in reality change the mapping of our brains and the functionality of our performance (Donald L. Hilton). We see examples of this in our society, in our communities, and perhaps in our own families. People that you once knew and could communicate with change drastically. I've asked myself many times if it is my perspective of that person that has changed, or is it the change that occurred within them? I believe it is both, but based on addiction, there is no doubt that the person will change due to what is happening inside the brain.

When analysis is performed in regards to what an addiction is, one really must note that it is a part of the mind. Addiction will often manifest itself in the form of the body, and ultimately becomes a defining aspect for the person. Perhaps that is why it is so difficult for a person to overcome and then turn away from the addiction. They would be turning away from themselves...from the person they created. Even when people are miserable in their addiction, they continue because it becomes who they are and it is also true what they say; misery loves company. Not only will desire change, but the brain will change (Donald L. Hilton). All of this due to what a person is feeding their brain, from the thought, to the way they will plan and scheme how to obtain their addiction.

Chapter 10

In 1921, a young college student argued with a professor about the existence of God. He spoke about how words are categorized to create meaning but in reality may not be correct. He pointed out that darkness is not the opposite of light, but that it is the absence of light, because in reality we cannot make dark darker. Mankind has created these meanings to make sense of what they experience. This young student was Albert Einstein and this lead him to write a book titled God vs. Science.

It is not proof that drives mankind, it is faith. Though faith is hard at times to explain, or even understand; we can choose to believe or to be a person without belief. Apply this truth to personal success and accountability and what becomes of your reasoning? Are you successful? How do you choose to see yourself? Again, are you successful or are you a person without success? That question and all other truths are tucked away deep in our minds. When we change the thought, we create a new character. Through thought refinement and guided action, we can create whatever success we desire.

I begin this chapter with that story of Albert Einstein because he is one of the greatest minds that ever lived. His quest and focus was to find information and explore its application in all areas. His contributions are still benefiting our world a hundred years after his death. There are many proposed theories that might explain how we came to be and why we are here. For the purpose of bringing additional light to success and how success is created, I would like to use the three most common creation methods: The Creation, The Big Bang Theory, and Evolution. My goal in this chapter will be to point out each and the relation that they have with success.

Creation – Creating success is a process, much like creating the world was a process. The Bible points out that God created Heaven and Earth in a period of 6 days and rested on the 7th day (Genesis 1:1-31;2:1-3). Though we may not know the exact time frame of these "days" or what exactly occurred, we know that at the end, God declared that it was good and was able to rest. One observation comes from the saying, "all work and no play makes Jack a dull boy." Insert your name for Jack and the word undesirable for dull.

Rest completes us; it just needs to be in moderation. If anything, I feel like our society could benefit from more work and less play, but those of you reading are not those to whom I am referring. Current statistics reveal that 58% of people never read a book after high school, and 42% of people never read a book after college (National Endowment for Arts – To Read or Not to Read, A Question of National Consequence). You who are reading represent a small percentage of people who choose to be uncommon, different, and educated. As we discussed earlier in the book, the ability to succeed is tied to the ability to read.

I want to delve further into the language and description

used. He commanded the elements through the language "Let there be" and the elements obeyed. Our current understanding may paint the picture that this language is demanding (Genesis 1:3,6,9,11,14-15,20,24,26). However, in looking at the root of the Hebrew words, we find that the elements actually desired to follow instruction. Similarly in our own lives, we must learn to create success and goodness through the knowledge that we are not intended to fail. Though you may not know it now, I hope it is becoming increasingly clear that success is not an accident, much like accountability is not chance. It is a choice!

Because we choose what we think, we choose what the outcomes will be. Will there be surprises? No doubt, but again by our response we choose to be positive or negative. Positivity alone is a success and identifies an attitude of self-confidence and security. Positivity is displayed by choice and is definitely the road less traveled in today's society. The easy road is negativity and choosing to be unhappy or upset simply because the life around us is difficult, we encounter hardships, and life is unfair.

Though these statements are true it does not mean that they are right or should be a way of life. We have over 20,000 thoughts per day and unfortunately over 50% of those are negative (Daniel Kahneman). What could you do if you believed rather than feared? What would you over about yourself if you chose to look for good in people and in the world? Negativity depresses, it debilitates, and it causes fear.

Creating success is built upon the premise that you use

what you have, the resources around you, and you discover that through a process, your end result is growth. Success is built around identifying a purpose, setting goals or outlining the performance, and then working and adjusting until we obtain. Even if it takes longer than we thought, if things are more difficult than expected, or we encounter the illusion of impossibility, Audrey Hepburn said it best; "Nothing is impossible, the word itself says I'm possible!"

We create the success we desire by the thoughts we hold most dear. Success is a creation based process and our thoughts, actions, words, and character will eventually determine our end result. Success, however, is not necessarily monetarily alone; it is not fame or fortune. Success is the declaration that it is good at the end of a process, journey, or battle and we are able to rest. Success is treating people fairly, giving dignity and respect to all, regardless of whether we think they deserve it or not.

Finally success is looking yourself in the eye at the end of each day and knowing you gave your best and though it was a struggle, you will do better tomorrow. Success or your attitude represents the part that you do not give up, give in, or shrink. Perhaps the best way to look at success might just be happiness. The relative property that connects success and happiness, as with everything, is the choice to think it, believe it, and be it.

The Big Bang Theory revolves around elements traveling in random motion, and as they collided they formed what we know of as the Earth, the moon, the stars, and all we know (http://www.umich.edu/~gs265/bigbang.

htm). The collision was one of massive proportions, and through perfect disorder became perfect order. Such is the life perhaps of someone each of us may know. That for some reason or another and despite the odds, success just exploded onto their landscape. Funny things can happen when preparation and luck meet (Oprah Winfrey).

Contrary to the saying that lightning only strikes once, though we may not see it, lightning and people strike (succeed) many times in life (NSSL). According to the National Severe Storm Laboratory (NSSL), lightning actually strikes the same place many times. Often times this happens in the same storm. The Empire State Building gets struck by lightning dozens of times per year. My comparison is that a person's success may look like dumb luck or "random motion" to the onlooker, but there is much more involved than one person's genius in regards to a successful outcome.

The other observation that I would like to make that relates to success is that lightning bolts are created by a negative charge separating from the clouds and as they begin heading toward the ground, the negative electrons are met by positive charges moving upwards. This intersection of opposites creates a channel and lightning is created. Success does not come from only experiencing the good. Success is learning how to work with the negative, while fostering the positive.

Similar to lightning, success and happiness is a mix of both. As with the example of The Big Bang Theory, elements that collide can and often do create beautiful things. Those who have obtained any level of success have done so by passing through the good and the bad, or having a collision course with both the good and the bad. From an outside perspective, we may only see another person's success as undeserved luck or perhaps we say "why can't I just be lucky?" or even "only good things happen for them."

We can all be assured that there is someone in the world who has it worse than we do and gratitude will help us eliminate these fleeting thoughts with the assurance that we have it very good. Specifically, we do not know what the person encountered within their mind or their environment that had to be overcome. Even if we don't know anyone personally that supposedly has it worse than we do, if we look long and hard enough we can find whatever we desire, if we are also willing to work. Additionally, we must understand that the trials of life are not always given randomly like people in a cafeteria gathering food. We must understand very clearly that we have been the cause for some if not many of the trials we face. Our choice, our decisions, our thoughts will contribute to our happiness of misery. You choose!

The final observation that I would call to your attention to is the thought that we do not have to understand something completely before we accept it. Just because we don't see it doesn't mean we cannot believe. I cannot explain how in milliseconds the process of lightning happens. However, I know that there are people who do understand lightning and can explain it well. Additionally, I have come to know that thunder will serve as a reminder that lightning is near. Look for those things in life that serve as a reminder for you to take cover and seek shelter. Like the darkest night happens just before the dawn, reminders help to educate and will provide learning.

Let us remember that we do not know everything. At times we may think we know everything, or talk like we know everything, or even act like we know everything, but we can all be assured that this is false. I am confident that if we think hard enough, we can all recall a time that we have been wrong. If not, your time is coming soon. Knowledge and understanding is a beautiful thing and there is more than a lifetime's worth to accumulate. The only limits that exist in reality are the ones we set ourselves. Truly, our minds have limitless power and capabilities. Realize that bodies can limit progress, but most often it is the inability to understand just how amazing you are. Do not set limits on yourself, but seek to discover and evolve into greatness.

Evolution takes into account all that we know from science and data and provides the knowledge that over time organisms adapt to their environment (Charles Darwin). This adaptation is the evolutionary process that happens so that elements are fit to survive in their environment. Success is no different. We come to this world with certain traits, skills, and resources. Depending upon many factors that are always in an evolutionary state themselves, we begin to develop or evolve into who we ultimately become.

Many studies point to the fact that much of a child's confidence is based on what a mother teaches the child and how she refers to the child (Laura E. Berk – Child Development). Additionally, there is no doubt that a father figure is essential for a child's development as well as the friends that each of us have and then of course our choices. Furthermore, we define ourselves by the activities that we choose, the music we listen to, the books we read, and the choice to become. As children we believe that we can become anything, but as adults we tend to struggle with that concept.

Regardless of the environment, we progressively choose what we choose based on the evolution of what we think will make us happy, safe, and/or improve our situation. We have been given five senses not by chance, but to aid us in our development. We learn by these senses to respond to the world around us. Even though not everyone is guaranteed all senses, the power to feel, combined with the intelligence to think, will provide clarity to even the most difficult of situations.

When we reflect back on Maslow's Hierarchy of Needs, we begin to see clarity based on how we, as well as others, make choices. Evolution, especially when considering human development, asks the question "what is important to you?" That can be further broken down into needs vs. wants. What a person chooses may not always reflect what they need, but can indicate clearly what they want. The same can be said about choosing what we need and forgoing what we want. Clearly, there becomes a natural classification for choice, which is thought. Thought is the root of choice and will lead people through the evolution from mental (thought) to physical (action) that they will eventually obtain.

It is self-evident that as youth, or in certain situations, choices are made by others that will affect personal choice. All of us have experienced this many times in life. This also serves as highly important to our evolution. We will eventually need to think for ourselves and act according to our own dictates. It is important for personal development, but it is even more essential for accountability.

Often times people get into such a habit of allowing others to tell them what they should do that they rely completely on others to make decisions for them. They say, "Well what do you think I should do?" or "I don't know what to do," or my personal favorite, "What would you do if you were me?"

Perhaps this is why we all seek to be understood, accepted, and validated. Now let me clarify something before you cast the stones of disbelief. It is very important for us to have a person or people in our lives who can listen and serve as a resounding voice of reason and helpful advice. Too often, this role is taken by someone who may tell you what to do, without knowing what is best for you, or they will make the decision based on what they think is best for you.

In my own life, I have seen this progression as I confided in others. There have been many times where I have had to simply stop asking and start thinking. We all have the power and resources we need to obtain anything that we desire. Though it may take time, though it may be uncomfortable, and it is a guarantee that you will make some wrong decisions along the way, choose to learn rather than repeat. Our progress in anything is best defined by personal choice and accountability. Perhaps you ask others how to proceed so that if and when it doesn't work, you have someone to blame? Seek understanding from the best sources, but when it comes down to it, you make the decision with confidence and assurance.

Success is not about repeating harmful, stressful, or problematic things day in and day out. It is to look at a situation and think about what we have learned, what we know, and what we desire in the form of results. We must also learn from others and be observant to the world around us. There is not enough time to make all the mistakes. The foundation for accountability is learning to trust our decisions and make them based on a set of standards, rules, laws, performances, etc. We seldom learn the valuable lessons when we live life on auto pilot and allow others that sacred right.

The evolution of success is similar in power to the evolution of choice. Over time, adaptation will occur and this is based on the environmental circumstances that we all encounter. The best training for learning is exposure, research, and application. Like the test that was never studied for, how can you make a decision without knowing what you need and/or want? The reason I refer to choice as a sacred right is that we are eventually defined by our choices as they become our habits. Why would we give this away to another? How will anyone treat the decisions in your life as delicately as you would if you were to make them on your own? I submit that there are few people who can make decisions for others in purity.

Consult with trusted mentors and advisors, but do not let that decision out of your sight. Great decisions come when a person considers three things: what is right, what is important, and is it a need? I categorize them this way because that will bring your heart, your mind, and your goals in one place. If you can align your heart with your mind and include your goals, you will no doubt make good, then better, and finally the best decisions to find success. This is not like a diet or short term "give it a shot"; this is a lifestyle and a commitment. By changing the way we look at decisions, we can have more assurance that our thinking will be supported by thoughts that reflect our goals, dreams, and desires.

In my own life, I decided to take on a challenge that would both push me to my limits and make me work for something that is outside the norm. I decided to compete in an NPC (National Physique Committee) competition. This decision is partly based on my desire to be in the best shape of my life. This was a goal that I set at the first of the year and saw that I needed to make a drastic change as I continued to plateau. My other reason was partly to honor my grandfather, Moroni Schwab. He competed and won the 1947 Mr. Utah competition. In 1948 he took 3rd place in Mr. America and in 1949 he took 8th place in Mr. Universe body building competitions. Additionally he served in the United States Navy and played professional football for the New York Bulldogs in 1950. He is still living at 90 years old, and he and my grandma have always been great examples of hard work, persistence, and accountability.

Moroni Schwab

The regimen was something of extreme difficulty. I have tried to maintain good health since my twenties and have been stuck in the category of athletic, but not "show ready." To be show ready I had to monitor my eating on a daily basis. I had to report, or hold myself accountable to a trainer. Sending pictures with my shirt off was uncomfortable for me. I also had to send daily reports showing what I ate and drank. I began this journey much like other things I have tried. I was just doing what I had always done. However, I have found that doing what I always have done will give me the results I have always had (Mark Twain).

As my trainer noticed my resistance to change, we had a very straightforward talk. He said, "If you're serious about this, you need to clean it up! No more dairy and no more sugar. Get disciplined." That was the tipping point and from that time forward I worked my guts out at the gym on a daily basis and I have eaten cleaner than I have ever eaten. I have found that I am happier and have much more energy. I didn't think that I was doing that bad. In retrospect, I really wasn't doing that bad. However, to compete at a higher level, I had to increase my level of accountability.

I now understand more fully how weight gets away from people. I own a supplement and smoothie business and I thought I knew health pretty well. It turns out we can all use a healthy dose of rearranging our focus and making accountable changes. I went through the process of creating new habits of success. I also found my body evolving based on the habits I was creating. Finally, through a series of disorders to my schedule, I found order. My goal was simply to be "show ready." What I gained is a healthier body, mind, and soul. I have also found success based on being happier, having more energy, and living with a clear purpose when it comes to my food and beverage consumption.

So now, what can be learned from the three creation examples and how they apply to success? My hope is that one or all of these speaks to you and you can identify this as your truth or representative of your perspective. If none of these examples work for you, the best way is to create what makes the most sense to you and what you can agree with. Personally, both with the creation of the world and the creation of success, I believe that all things are created spiritually, then mentally before they are created physically.

Regardless of how the world was created and how each of us creates our own success, there must be a defined goal and performance that leads to attainment. Performance will not be seamless, nor will we be right every time, but with a dedication that leads to the attainment of that goal, we arrive at the unquestionable point of success. Learn to be patient with yourself and know that you do not have all the information just yet. The joy in the journey, as some refer to life, is choosing to learn along the way rather than always looking in the rear view mirror of 20/20 understanding. Trust your feelings and proceed with the faith that you can and you will succeed.

> "You can't connect the dots looking forward, you can only connect them looking backwards. So you have to trust that the dots will somehow connect in your future. You have to trust in something – your gut, destiny, life, karma, whatever."
>
> -*Steve Jobs*-

Success is a destination that begins with small steps that create consistency. Consistency is important, but we can also be consistently negative or have poor results that are consistent. Why? If things aren't going as you would hope, do you stop to think through the challenge or the direction you are taking? Do not accept status quo, average, or ok. You deserve the best, but the best will require more than you are currently doing! What you are currently doing has you in the situations that you are currently in. Though some of these may be random events, it is time to take back your life and be brilliant, healthy, and happy because you make the choice and reinforce the choice with everything you think and everything you choose.

I assure you that nobody has a perfect life free from challenge, but people do have the life that they want. If that is not true then why don't people change their life? Too hard... not enough time....bad job....no education.... something happened in the past that doesn't allow your happiness? Whatever your perspective is will probably determine how you look at these insensitive but true statements. There is sadness, trials, unfortunate events, the terrible, but it is not permanent unless you decide that it is. Consider this quote: "I will arrive at my destination only when I know exactly where it is" (Author Unknown).

Obviously people don't wake in the morning and think, "I can't wait to be miserable today." Our attitude, however, does begin with the choice of what we want the day to be. Will the day be a success or the absence of success?

That is completely up to the attitude of the individual and how they get out of bed, what they do to get their day going, and how they manage their time. If we look at the day and assess what must be done and compare that with the total time we have for the day, we can begin adding things that contribute to our dreams, goals, and desires. We can then remove those things that are unneeded, undesirable, and a waste of time.

A personal inventory takes the total of something, subtracts the mandatory responsibilities, and then we have blocks of time that need a choice. Will we watch TV, surf the web, sleep, hang out with friends? Remember these are all choices and will contribute to our overall happiness or sadness. As we discussed earlier in the book, accomplishment will require individuals to sacrifice and to create alternatives for time that we may not think currently exist. To sacrifice is to push ourselves out of the comfort zone and into areas of life that demand new thought, new action, and new beginnings. Sacrifice provides the hope that with a little more work, we can become our hope.

Now, if your day is so packed full of things, realistically could some of those things be eliminated? Could you wake up earlier or stay up a little later? Sleep is essential, but if you had less what could you do with the time? Do not use "can't" as you think about your time. Can't will eliminate your creative processing that will provide answers when you ponder through any circumstance. Can't more often than not is an excuse for "I don't want" or "I am not really in the mood" or "I think smaller than I could be." Whatever the reason for using can't, find times in your day that you can replace with the most essential. Improve your life on a daily basis on purpose.

You may not even know it, but I would imagine that there are times during your day or week that you waste. Even the most dedicated person will waste time. If it is something that is here and there, I would not be too stressed about micro-managing your day or week. However, if hours are spent on social media, on the phone, or watching TV, unless this is your job and you are paid for it, then it could probably be reduced. Remember to approach each day with accountability for reason, success, and for brilliance. Manage your time like it is the most essential asset that you have because it is. We all have the same amount of time in a day; use your time to the fullest to pursue dreams, goals, and greatness.

These are suggestions, and I am making general statements. However, introspection is needed in your life to challenge that comfortable feeling that everything is just fine while in your mind you are communicating a different story. The lack of consistency is what causes the misery, and it is misery that loves company. Make the decision to relocate your summer home on misery lane to the address of your dreams by making the choice to do more and live great. You know work is required, but don't let that scare you off. You may not be happy right now, but also understand that you have the power to create change, and through change will come happiness and success.

If you don't know how to take the first step, find someone who is visibly happy or in your mind successful, and ask them how they obtained what they have. As time marches on, happiness to some will be weird or peculiar or even the thought might be unobtainable. However, do not let the thoughts of some influence your thoughts. Make the decision, adjust your attitude, have dreams and goals, and work toward attainment. I spoke with a sports psychologist recently who raised my level of thinking and ultimately performance (Craig Manning – The Fearless Mind). Dr. Manning spoke about when we live in the past; it often is attended with guilt. If we live in the future, we often live with fear. We must live in the present with just enough view of the future and the understanding of where we are going and what we desire to become.

Example 10.1

As we have talked thoroughly about the concept of accountability throughout the book, the taking of personal responsibility is the foundational principle. Any process requires a different way of doing, it requires being. One aspect that we have talked about in depth throughout the book is to have an attitude of gratitude. Whether you have the belief in a higher power, energy, no belief, or just a firm belief in yourself, success is not just built by a one man team. It is a combination of the efforts of many. Parents, teachers, community, mentors, friends, and many other interactions help define ourselves, our ideas, and provide the guidance for what we will become.

Consider the benefits of gratitude as a way to take the focus off yourself and recognize the resources all around you. Often times we look at a goal or something we need to do as a personal quest. However, when we have gratitude for all we have, we will begin identifying others who can assist and resources that will help us persist. We begin to recognize others and helpful resources that we fail to see when the focus is on self-fulfillment and solo task completion. Let me be clear in that I am not saying to shift the responsibility to others to help us get what we want. I am saying that as we take the personal responsibility of getting started, not quitting, and most importantly, being grateful, we eliminate some of the pressures and stress of having to do everything ourselves.

By tapping into resources and working with people, like a well of water, we establish a consistent source that can be drawn from time after time. Do not let the past experiences of negativity and pain to dictate the future opportunities for perspective, growth, and attainment. Allowing others to help often times is deeply seated based on past disappointment, learning to make it on your own, or trust. Trust is real and often times is directly associated with learning and doing. Forgiveness is a trait that can and will restore trust in self and others. Use both trust and forgiveness graciously and work to forgive past hurt, misunderstanding, broken trust, and ultimately sadness.

Regardless of people or resources, we still have to be the driving force behind what we desire. Having people and resources speeds up the process and gives a clear direction toward accomplishment. Gratitude is the foundation for additional opportunity simply because we interrupt the normal pattern created when we have to have control. If we have an attitude of gratitude we learn to get out of the way and see the contributions of others, while balancing the project as a director, not a dictator.

Exercise 10.1

Stop and take a moment to do the exercise below. This is a step by step process of identifying the what, why, and how of your success.

What (the success): Define the success that you desire. This can be done in the form of a declaration or goal, but know that it does not become real until you write it down. Writing it down brings what we want into reality. Remember that we are looking to align our subconscious (spiritual) with our conscious (mental).

Why (the reason): Why is this so important? If it isn't important then don't worry about it and stop talking about how you will do this or do that. If something is important you will take the time to think it through, write it down, and work your guts out until you succeed. This is also a great time to identify excuses and eliminate them.

How (the process): Begin with gratitude for all you have and based on your "what" and "why," you have the confidence to act (physical) and obtain the how. Realize that the how is a process and will take time, faith, and adjustments. I will add one more that will take you to a new level of attainment. The goals or declarations need to be said aloud with conviction daily, once in the morning and once in the evening.

For me, these were the very steps that I took in writing this book and here is my what, why, and how.

What: Write a book that gets published.

Why: To do something that I have always dreamed of doing. To develop myself by recording my thoughts and putting into action my feelings. To change the world, even if it is just one person.

How: Begin with just a couple of sentences per day to establish consistency. Adjust the input based on what I want the output to be. Eliminate self-pity, self-doubt, and self-defeating thoughts. Collect the material from everything I have read, all that I think, and interactions with others that have increased my perspective. Write the book for what people need to hear, not what they want to hear.

Society, community, parents, friends, etc. will define success in different ways, but it is essential that you make the decision of how you define success. Once we have defined it, we then take the necessary steps to progress through the process of a lifetime. Some success is short-term, while other successes are long-term. Making the choice of what is important to you as an individual and having the goals to get there will give you a life of meaning that is created by you.

If we develop the attitude of gratitude and observe the world around us, we begin to see ways that we can help and contribute on a higher level.

A quote that provides additional meaning here is: "If your actions inspire others to dream more, learn more, do more, and become more, you are a leader" (John Quincy Adams). Success is not just about taking care of your own needs or wants. We learn that as we create success, it includes the world and people around us. Through communication, we learn, develop, and enjoy more success. Through success we find confidence, purpose, and opportunity.

Example 10.2

Nobel Prize recipient Roger Sperry introduced a concept known as the Cognitive Preference Index or CPI (http://www.nobelprize.org/nobel_prizes/medicine/laureates/1981/sperry-lecture_en.html). It will help clarify additional points as we seek to better understand ourselves, our decision making, and our results.

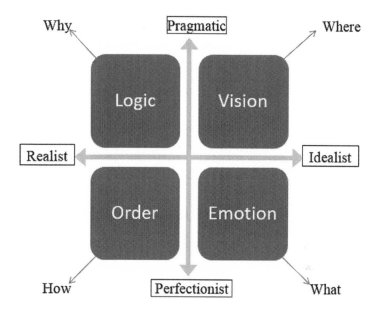

Proficiency comes with time, dedication, and balance. Most people are strong in only two of these areas. It is possible that a person can have a third area of strength. Generally, a person has two areas that they are strongest, which clearly identifies who they are and how they make decisions. Where are you strong? As you combine the two areas for strength are you pragmatic, an idealist, a perfectionist, or a realist? Knowing your strengths is a good predictor of what will make you successful. This model captures human behavior in terms that are understandable and will bring a new level of recognition to ourselves and others.

Success takes who we are, pairs it with what we know, and challenges us with what we must become. Success can seem like it is overwhelming or that it may take something that we may not have. Overwhelming feelings are a way to monitor your progress. If you never step out of your comfort zone, you will not progress. However, if you continually stack on loads of lists, goals, and items to obtain you may feel the stress that shuts a person down. Only you can know how much you can give. I want you to raise your hand as high as you can right now. If you are actually doing this, I applaud you; now raise it one more inch. I have seen this example play out in groups and have always found that even when told to raise your hand as high as you can, that you can raise it one more inch.

Such is life, goal setting, and success. We will be stretched and we will feel that we have nothing left to give. However, is that any different than the feelings you have had before when encountering hardship? People learn to push through because they have to. Think of a relationship, or work, or challenge that you have overcome before. Now apply that to the success that you desire. When you hit a roadblock, push through, climb over, go around, or simply lift the roadblock. What you think you can or cannot do will be manifested in your physical ability to take the first step. Throughout this book and now hopefully the rest of your life, I have endeavored to place the highest level of importance on thought, thought control, and thought development. Now is the time to bring your thoughts in line with your actions. Now go and do!

Afterword

Over the course of this past year, I have encountered so many challenges that have changed the way I look at life. I have had situations that have literally brought me to my knees in weakness time and time again. I have been through possibly the hardest times that I have ever encountered in my life. The difficulty of writing this book fails to even compare with life's events over the past year. However, the difficulty of writing this book is the very thing that saved me from sinking into a depressed state of mind. If not for a wonderful wife and family I could not say that I would have completed this book or lived accountably. Without accountability I can declare that I would not have enjoyed happiness.

Life is about progression and if you think you have nothing to offer, I challenge you to start building. Little steps or successes can be a powerful anti-depressant.

Accountability is that step by step process that each of us must take. However, I also understand that accountability does not eliminate reality. The reality is that life is hard and we will get angry and have negative thoughts. When we live accountably it does not magically make life easier, but it does give life meaning, creates additional purpose, and will allow for a clear perspective. Accountability is simply holding oneself answerable. Answerable to whom? That is for you to decide based on what is important to you and who you desire to become. Make the decision once so confusion doesn't sway you in moments where feelings or emotions give tunnel vision.

We will all have to answer to someone at some point in this life or beyond. Why not start now by holding ourselves accountable to our thoughts, our words, our actions, our habits, and our character? I do not believe that simply being exposed to environments determines who we must be or will give us the excuse that we are justified or entitled. Facing the difficulties of justification will help us find happiness like we have never before felt. Though something may be common or natural in society, it does not mean that it is right or empowering. I know nothing more empowering than facing each day, week, month, and year with the determination to be great despite. Despite challenge, unfortunate events, disease, death, brutality, and anything that life will present to us.

Accountability is the choice that empowers greatness. When we choose not to be accountable, we choose the highway of life that most people travel. Those who are looking for someone else to choose for them or someone to deliver them, unfortunately, will not find accountability and therefore their happiness is in jeopardy. True and lasting happiness comes when we understand who we are and, no matter what, we are true to that understanding. Misery comes when life is lived inconsistently compared to what we feel is right or by choosing to blame everyone but ourselves. When pointing the finger of blame, realize that we usually have three pointing back at us.

My approach was to give a different perspective and I

hope that I accomplished that. Even if I challenged what you believe or feel to be right, I hope that the generated thoughts served as a compass to align you with that place where you want to go. Regardless of whether you take a train, a boat, a car, or have to walk, your journey will begin and end with accountability. Do not be surprised if, when you choose to be accountable, you encounter the odds and difficulties that will make you want to quit. In quitting you learn nothing and it also becomes a habit.

It is so common in life to be able to see lessons or things in others, but I challenge you to look in the mirror and discover you probably have weaknesses and character flaws that must be recognized. Not for the purpose of being negative or to create a built-in excuse, but to know that we too have faults and that we must work on self before we can work on others. This work is the work of a lifetime and the challenge that we all must face.

How can I be accountable? Even when we discover this on a personal level, we can always improve, and by observing ourselves and others, we will learn what needs to be done to clean house. The biggest journey is not denying ourselves of thought. Our thoughts will tell everything about who we truly are. Whether they boil under the surface or find their way into our character, we will eventually encounter our thoughts as words, actions and inactions, habits, and character. It is imperative that we break down who we are into thought. Once we recognize the source, we can understand how to adjust and proceed to discover more about ourselves and where we are going.

Because we can control our thoughts, we can control who

we are and who we will become. If you do not currently like the thoughts that you have, change them. That may be easier said than done, but nothing that is worth it will be easy. If you are looking for easy, then accountability may not be for you? My experience with accountability has been a choice that continually challenges me to seek out what is most important. Even if there are two good choices, weigh the choices against the most accountable and it will serve us in the short term and the long term. As we create consistency within accountability, we create happiness.

I would love to hear from you. Whether you agree or disagree, I believe that through discussion and debate we learn and can come to understand perspective better. As we understand someone better, though it may not change our mind, it will change our perspective. I want to thank my family and friends for encouraging me and keeping me accountable. When I initially said that I was going to write this book, I had intended to write a couple of chapters and have a ghost writer finish. Wow, that would have been interesting especially with the subject matter and book title. I am glad that I pushed through my initial limiting beliefs of "I have no time" or "I can't complete a task like this."

To my beautiful wife, I love you and thank you for living accountably and holding me accountable. My greatest hope is that we teach our children to be accountable no matter what. Accountability is not always convenient or comfortable; thank goodness that it is the driving force behind positive change. I am grateful that my wife let me play author even when she knew it would take place in the time we had together and the time I had to interact with our children. I want to thank my mentors and confidants; you push me based on the thoughts we have shared and your continual actions toward accountability. I would like to thank everyone I have ever had an interaction with. Whether it was good or bad, it taught me and brought me to today.

I would also like to thank employers and those for whom I did work and those who worked me. Not every working relationship always ends with what expectations were in the beginning. To my mom, one of my biggest supporters who has changed my world, I love you. To my first employer, my dad, who employed me and taught me to never quit, to the farm work that taught me no matter who is watching there is a job that needs to get done. To Kevin Stewart, who helped me see that work can be both fun and profitable and whom I view as another father. I have had the fortunate experience of working for free, doing jobs that have very little enjoyment, and work that ended before I would have hoped. Work carries with it the dual power to provide hope and create value.

For those on the planes and passengers I have met, thank you for letting me talk the whole time and be the resounding voice of what you thought or what you would like to read. Yeah, I am that guy that always talks to anyone who sits by me, so watch out. I want to make mention that though the editing is thorough, inevitably I will miss something or someone, so please don't take it personal. I am the composite of everyone who influenced me from Mrs. Grover my kindergarten teacher to my last professor Sandy Goff; you created my curiosity to grow and to explore.

For the authors who I read and love, thank you for teaching me the ability to look at life differently. I am drawn to self-help books and love the positive message that anything is possible. I am thankful that I have people in my life who, through a smile, hello, or "how you are doing?" pick me up and lift me to higher ground. Through communication with others I have gained a perspective that helps me to succeed even in the face of failure. I am thankful for the foundation that I am able to build upon based on parents, grandparents, community, leaders, and the motivational. We do not always understand what people are dealing with or the figurative or literal demons they face. Thank you for being happy anyway and fighting the fight.

Finally, I would like to leave myself and everyone who reads this book a personal challenge. Be accountable! Learn personally what it is, how it is applied, and then teach it to others. I have put my heart, my soul, and everything I could possibly give into this book. I challenge the accountable to live life the same way. Give your best because nothing else will do. Accountability is the successful way that we can change ourselves. We cannot change others, but through our lives, we gently prompt others to choose to change. If enough people hold themselves completely accountable, we will change the world. Do not quit. Even when you think you may have arrived at accountability, you must continue. Different forms, challenges, and options will present themselves around every corner and I hope that you and I can say with confidence: I am accountable and I lived each day with unconquerable dedication.

Citations

Chapter 1

Oprah Winfrey

Pg. 5

Winston Churchill

Pg. 9

Chapter 2

New York Times

Pg. 14

http://www.nytimes.com/2012/02/18/us/for-women-under-30-most-births-occur-outside-marriage.html?pagewanted=2&_r=0
?Remove www.unifiedfamilies.org Pg. 14- Dead link? Remove

National Institute of Health

Pg. 14

http://www.ncbi.nlm.nih.gov/pmc/articles/PMC2853053

Nielsen Report

Pg. 15

http://www.nielsen.com/content/corporate/us/en/newswire/2013.
html?q=television watching&sortbyScore=false&tag=Category%3AMedia+and+Entertainment

National Literacy Survey

Pg. 15

National Center for Education Statistics; Adult Literacy in America. U.S. Department of Education. Office of Educational Research and Improvement. NCES 1993-27

Michigan State

Pg. 15

http://msutoday.msu.edu/news/2004/children-spend-more-time-playing-video-games-than-watching-tv-msu-survey-shows/

Chapter 3

Chapter 4

Chapter 5

Chapter 8

Chapter 9

Gratitude and Well Being, Alex M. Wood, Jeffery J. Froh, and Adam W.A. Geraghty.

Pg. 114

Robert Duncan Quote,

Pg. 116

Salvo Magazine July 2010, Donald L. Hilton

Pgs. 119,125-126

http://www.salvomag.com/new/articles/salvo13/13hilton.php

Chapter 10

God Vs. Science, Albert Einstein

Pg. 127

Creation Process, Genesis 1:1-31; 2:1-3

Pg. 128

James Howell Quote

Pg. 128

To Read or Not to Read, A Question of National Consequence, NEA

Pg. 128

Let there be light, Genesis 1:3,6,9,11,14-15,20,24,26

Pg. 129

Daniel Kahneman, Negative Thoughts per day

Pg. 129

Audrey Hepburn Quote

Pg. 130

Big Bang Theory

Pg. 130

http://umich.edu/-gs265/bigbang.htm

Oprah Winfrey Quote

Pg. 131

Lightning Strikes, The National Severe Storm Laboratory (NSSL)

Pg. 131

Made in the USA
Coppell, TX
24 October 2019

10392891R00109